CW01512117

TROMBONI

Trombone Technique

DENIS WICK

Second Edition

Oxford   New York

OXFORD UNIVERSITY PRESS

Oxford University Press, Walton Street, Oxford OX2 6DP

Oxford New York Toronto
Delhi Bombay Calcutta Madras Karachi
Petaling Jaya Singapore Hong Kong Tokyo
Nairobi Dar es Salaam Cape Town
Melbourne Auckland

and associated companies in
Berlin Ibadan

Oxford is a trade mark of Oxford University Press

First published 1971
Second edition 1984
Reprinted with corrections 1989

ISBN 0 19 322378 3

Printed in Great Britain by
Caligraving Ltd, Thetford

Contents

INTRODUCTION

The trombone has for me always been a source of endless fascination. I hope it will remain so! Its enormous range of tone colour, its capacity to express so many kinds of musical emotion—solemnity, warmth, brilliance, brashness, nerve-chilling starkness, comfortable good humour, or even sheer comedy—give it a unique place in the orchestral palette.

It has always been—and will remain—a difficult instrument to play really well; it demands lasting devotion and needs a thoroughgoing musician behind it.

Trombones are found in almost every conceivable muscial combination providing an inimitable quality, whether it be the rasp of the Dixieland bass-line or the glow of the orchestral pianissimo chord. The instrument undoubtedly has a high place in the public attention. Even the most casual observer will recognize the trombone when he sees it in band or orchestra; cheerful familiarity with the 'sludge-pump' or 'kid-shifter' have endeared it to generations.

The last few decades have seen a big improvement in playing standards, and from the fine examples of a few pioneers, notably in the field of jazz—the late Tommy Dorsey and Glenn Miller come to mind—has come a changed attitude to the trombone in all realms of music. From being primarily a noise-maker, except in the hands of a very few good players, the trombone has now won universal acceptance as a subtle, expressive, and almost vocal instrument.

The embodiment of all these desirable features can be found in the many fine trombone sections in symphony orchestras on both sides of the Atlantic; the standard of studio trombonists is just as high, although their aims are very different. I believe that whatever his musical environment, the following pages will be of at least some use to every trombonist; even the very best performers may not be fully aware of the mechanics of playing. If they smooth the way for some students, help the older player who finds in mid-career that his playing has suddenly gone wrong, or even stimulate argument among trombonists, then I shall be satisfied.

1
THE INSTRUMENT

Choice of instrument

A trumpeter, horn-player, or tuba player might conceivably use the same instrument for band, symphony orchestra, dance band, jazz group, or any other form of work. For the trombonist, however, these fields have such different requirements that he must provide a different kind of sound for each of them. Each size of instrument needs a mouthpiece which is properly suited to it, and which will not necessarily suit any of the others.

Here are lists of the trombones recommended for various types of playing. They are all made by well-known manufacturers, and the choice of instrument is really more a question of taste (and cost!) than anything else.

Beginners: (medium bore) Conn 18H, 50H; Blessing B128; Besson 637; Holton "Collegiate"; Yamaha YSL354; King 606.

Symphony: (large bore) Conn 8H and 88H; 7H and 78H (medium/large); Bach 42 and 42B; Bach 36 and 36B (medium/large); Courtois CSL 200B, 300B; Blessing B8, B88; Besson 942 and 944: Holton TR 156, 158, 256, 258; Yamaha YSL 647, 648, 681, 682.

Dance band/Studio: King 2102, 2103; Bach 12, 16; Conn 6H, 100H; Holton TR100; Martin "Urbie Green" model; Yamaha YSL 645, 653, 691.

Jazz: King 2102; Holton TR100; Bach 12; Yamaha YSL 653.

Brass band: 1st trombone medium/large bore as above, 2nd trombone large bore instrument. Both Besson and Yamaha large bore trombones are rather easier to cope with than Bach, for instance, and have the kind of nimble response that suits modern brass band writing. They are equally to be recommended with medium/large trombones for 1st or 2nd.

Bass trombones: Bach 50B, 50B2, 50B3; Besson "Sovereign"; Conn 110H, 111H, 112H; Holton 181, 183; Yamaha YBL 322, 612, 613.

Alto trombones: Bach 39; Courtois CSL130; Latzsch; Glassl; Finke; Yamaha YSL 671.

When choosing an instrument for a young player, it is important to consider these main points:

(1) suitability of type of instrument
(2) quality of the instrument when new
(3) present condition of the instrument, regarding playing qualities, mechanical efficiency and appearance
(4) price

I can hardly over-emphasize the importance of securing the advice of a good player or teacher. Such a person will almost certainly advise the selection of a second—or for that matter tenth-hand good-quality trombone, provided that it is in good working order. This is invariably a better choice than a cheaply-made, shining, polished, and lacquered instrument of low quality which will depreciate in value very quickly.

Assuming that the beginner has already begun playing, possibly on a school instrument, so that he is not a complete novice, then the most economic purchase would be a medium-bore top-class instrument. This would last until he becomes competent enough to use a professional, large-bore symphony trombone. (If he does not get that far, then he need never buy another trombone.) If his career points towards lighter music, then this first purchase will take him all the way!

The general condition of the trombone should be carefully checked. If the bell is held 3 inches below the bell-stay at a point where it is about 2.5 inches in diameter, and rotated gently, previously invisible irregularities in its shape may appear, indicating that possibly many generations of dents have been removed, thereby stretching the metal. A good check on the slide is to hold the instrument vertically with the unlocked slide touching the floor. Raising the left hand will show if the slide is sticking. Dents in the outer slide—more readily detected through a piece of thin, silky cloth—may be quite easily removed by a good repairer (often hard to find). If the slides are 'out of true', a professional repair is necessary to line them up again. Worn plating on the inner slides usually indicates heavy wear on the softer outer slides. In this case, repair is difficult, if not impossible, and the parts generally need to be replaced. If this is the case, it would be better to look for another instrument. With the slide section detached, place the thumbs over the ends and hold in a vertical position with the outer slide released. The outer slide section should fall very slowly if the slide is reasonably airtight. Always check the slide action in the playing position as well as vertically. Do this first of all dry, then again when lubricated with cold cream and water (see page 1).

Playing tests

Check the intonation carefully, making sure that the middle and upper Fs are not too sharp or the D above middle C and high Bb too flat. Careful selection and fitting of the mouthpiece can minimize this problem. Most trombones have two notes that are likely to give trouble, high Ab, and top D. Make sure that they 'ring' and have no tendency to rattle or crack.

When trying a trombone with an F valve, make sure that the marks on the inner valve-casing line up. If they do not, it is a comparatively simple matter to fit new corks. A badly-fitted rotary valve can make a trombone feel very 'stuffy' and can needlessly prejudice the player against it.

A well played, well used trombone is always to be recommended, provided that it is not worn in the way I have described. A new trombone may not, at first acquaintance, reveal its full potential. It may need up to six months' use to 'run it in', to develop a rich sound and all-round smoothness. New instruments usually have a rawness and roughness about them that should to some extent be disregarded.

Choice of mouthpiece

Although there is a mystique about mouthpieces which makes even the most experienced players and teachers hesitate to give a definite opinion, I feel that I should at least offer mine, controversial though it may be, based on the experience which I have been able to gather.

Some mouthpiece characteristics are related to the individual player. Most, however, relate to the instrument with which they are to be used. These are: cup depth, cup curvature, and breadth; shoulder, and taper of throat, taper of back bore, and—very important—distance of projection. Personal considerations are the diameter of the cup and the shape of the rim. Even these personal preferences for a particular rim-shape or cup size can be carried too far. Human flesh can adapt to almost anything!

A wide range of mouthpieces is available today. Each manufacturer supplies with each of his instruments a mouthpiece often described as 'scientifically designed' or 'acoustically matched'. Many of the mouthpieces unfortunately prove not to be good enough for professional players. It is worth realizing that at least 90 per cent of the production of most makers goes to amateurs, schools, brass bands, and the like; it is only natural that the mouthpiece supplied with a particular trombone should be as easy and responsive as possible for a beginner. The ultimate potential of a trombone can rarely be achieved with a stock mouthpiece, even in the hands of a good professional player—usually the lower register and upper dynamic levels suffer considerably.

Most professional trombonists either use a mouthpiece which they have adapted from such a stock model, or go to a specialist mouthpiece-making company to select what is for them the ideal mouthpiece, depending upon the instrument they use and the work they have to do.

The Vincent Bach Corporation of Elkhart, Indiana, carries a stock of several hundred mouthpieces of different sizes and for every brass instrument. Whereas one can only applaud the enterprise and expertise that have made this possible, such a wide choice of mouthpieces puts before the student or young player endless temptations to change and experiment. Each model has a tempting description that sounds to the unsuspecting purchaser as if it could solve all his problems! Of course this cannot be true. In point of fact, there are too few sizes that are near to what most modern orchestral players use (about $1-1\frac{1}{32}$in. cup diameter) and a multiplicity of smaller sizes which suit medium-bore trombones most of which were designed in the 1920s.

There are also other mouthpiece companies who cater for

specialist requirements.* I have myself designed a range of trombone mouthpieces which are suitable for orchestral and band playing.† I have found that, once a workable rim and cup shape are established, with care given to the rim so that the highest point is towards the inner edge of the mouthpiece and the inner edge itself is not too sharp, these 'personal' considerations can be considered as standard as the cup throat and backbore. In this way I have solved the problems for myself and many British players, and have made a range of mouthpieces for all purposes which are intended, above all else, to give a full rich even tone throughout the entire register of the trombone, and to offer the best intonation compromise.

Suggested choices of mouthpiece

(1) *Beginners*: 9BS, 6BS or Bach 6½ AL
(2) *Brass band*: 9BS, 6BS, 5BS; or large-bore fitting: 6BL, 5BL, 4BL, Bach 6½AL, 5
(3) *Orchesral* (large bore) 6BL, 5BL, 5AL, 4½BL, 4½AL, 4BL, 4AL; Bach 6½AL, 5G, 4G
(4) *Dance band*: 7CS, 10CS, 12CS, Bach 11C, 12C

Still the best advice one can give to a young player is to seek the help and guidance of a good teacher to find a good mouthpiece, making sure that it suits first the instrument, then himself, then to stick to it! It is a good idea to keep two identical mouthpieces, just in case of accidental loss.

Mouthpieces which should be identical very often differ when any abrasive polishing is involved in the manufacture. Although the differences may be very small indeed—as little as .001 in.—the embouchure is quite capable of detecting this. It is therefore essential to heed the above advice, and *never* to change mouthpieces except in an emergency. For those trombonists who have for any reason to use alternatively a medium-bore and large-bore instrument, or a tenor and alto, the best solution is to use a screw rim combination mouthpiece.

---

*Such as Renold Schilke of Chicago and R. Gardinelli of New York
†Now sold by Boosey & Hawkes Ltd.

Most good mouthpiece makers will supply, for a comparatively small extra charge, a combination of two cups and one rim, so that each cup throat and backbore suits the instrument for which it is designed and the rim suits the player.

Finally, the mouthpiece *must* fit properly. Too much projection can make the flat-tending notes too flat in relation to the other notes on the instrument, too little projection may cause the sharp-tending notes to be too sharp. A good compromise, with just the right amount of projection, will not only give the best intonation, but also seems to make the trombone respond better generally.

For dance-music—clear, high register playing—select a smaller cup diameter ($3\frac{1}{32}$in. or 24.5mm) with narrow bore and fairly shallow cup. For band-playing and smaller orchestras, a slightly larger diameter (about 1 in.) and deeper cup. For large symphony orchestras, a rim diameter of not less than 1 in. and probably $1\frac{1}{64}$-$1\frac{1}{32}$in. (25.5-26mm) is to be advised, with a deep cup and larger throat and backbore (to be used in conjunction with large bore symphonic trombone).

For bass trombone, a cup diameter of $1\frac{1}{32}$-$1\frac{1}{16}$ inches (26.3-27mm) with a really deep cup should be selected.

To improve the high register, use a narrower, shallower cup, and smaller bore (this gives more 'edge', more precision, less roundness).

To improve the low register, use a larger bore, a deeper cup, and a wider cup diameter. This gives a darker sound.

Many players use mouthpieces that are too small, but are often reluctant to try a larger cup-diameter because they are afraid of losing their upper register. Once they have taken the plunge and changed to a bigger cup-diameter the weakness in the high register, which may indeed be expected, is quite short-lived. After a short time, in fact, the higher register may even be better than before. This is an added bonus to the increase in richness of sound, volume and flexibility which occur when such a change is made.

If this idea is carried to excess, and really large (bass trombone) mouthpieces are used with large-bore trombones, some highly undesirable results may be obtained. The large volume of sound thereby produced is naturally full, dark, and rich, and, while notes in the high register may project reasonably well, the timbre produced by an instrument so equipped at low dynamic levels is most uncharacteristic. Also, from the teacher's point of view, it is often difficult to detect embouchure faults if they are masked by the use of an over-large mouthpiece and I have often found it necessary to recommend a smaller one to some of my own students. One should always seek the advice of an experienced player, but as a general guide I would suggest a maximum diameter of 26mm. Assiduous long-note practice and the use of a metal practice mute can often improve tone quality to such an extent that the tone produced with a medium-sized mouthpiece usually surpasses that produced by an extra-large one, which can sound like a euphonium, and which encourages imperfect embouchure.

Many brass players prefer gold-plated mouthpieces because of the hypo-allergic properties and the appearance and extraordinarily 'soft' feel of gold-plating. I use this finish on my own mouthpieces, and find that the ultra-smooth surface helps flexibility. Any plating will, however, wear eventually: silver reacts to mouth acids, and although gold does not, it is much thinner than silver and much softer. When the plating gets worn, the mouthpiece *must* be replated, after the rim has been polished. Great care must be taken not to alter the contour of the rim during the polishing process.

German Trombones

Players of the German school use traditional instruments which have a completely different response, tone quality, and 'feel' from trombones made throughout the rest of the world. Although there are excellent trombonists in the great German orchestras, they often achieve their results in spite of their instruments, not because of them! For German trombones tend to have a soft, dull, warm quality of sound, which in loud playing 'breaks up' at a much lower dynamic level than, say, American instruments, which are more resonant at softer levels, and tend to maintain the same kind of tone quality from *ppp* to *fff*.

The bore size of German instruments is generally small, but bells are always very large—9 or 10 inches are not uncommon.

The metal used is generally softer, less work-hardened and 'springy' than other trombones, and the most noticeable characteristics are unwieldiness, heavy slide action, and a not particularly good high register. From these remarks it must be understood that although it is *possible* to play very well indeed on these instruments—many players have done so and still do —for the player who is used to a more manageable instrument they present problems. I should add, however, that international standards of instrument development and manufacture are constantly improving, and the present-day German instrument, which is actually the progenitor of the typical American symphony trombone, is already being 'Americanized' to give better slide action and balance.

The customary mouthpiece for use with the German-type trombone is rather small with a narrow bore. A mouthpiece of this type is needed not to provide roundness, solidity, and resonance, but to help the high register and generally to brighten the rather dull character of these instruments.

French trombones

The style of trombone-playing in France is unique, and although one may not like its rather narrow-bore sound with fairly continuous vibrato, one has to admit that there is an extremely high standard of playing and a wide recognition of the trombone as a solo instrument in France.

French trombonists naturally use instruments which fulfil their particular requirements. Thus we find that French trombones are traditionally light, small in bore and bell size, and very easy and responsive to play. They must be played with a smallish but fairly deep mouthpiece, and traditionally the French trombone mouthpiece is conical rather than cup-shaped.

American trombones

These are considered excellent from all points of view by a large majority of players and are used in every form of musical activity throughout the world. For suggested models see the list of recommended instruments on page 1.

British trombones

In Britain the many small firms that at one time competed in the manufacture of brass instruments have either disappeared altogether, or have now amalgamated with the Boosey & Hawkes group, the only British company now making trombones, but under the trade name 'Besson'.

In recent years the quality and design of Besson trombones have improved enormously. Their all-purpose instruments can now compare in ease of playing, sound quality, and workmanship with those of any other maker. Like musical instrument manufacturers throughout the world, Boosey & Hawkes have responded to the challenge of the Japanese Yamaha company, and the resulting competition to produce better trombones has meant improved quality, greater consistency, and in some cases, a wider choice of instruments. The new (1989) 942 and 944 large-bore Bessons are more responsive and easier to play than their American competitors. They also have a slightly more agreeable sound than similar Japanese models.

Japanese trombones

The enormous resources of the Yamaha company have brought about the design and manufacture of a whole range of trombones in various qualities from comparatively cheap beginners' instruments to expensive 'custom' models for professionals. By 1989 there were excellent models of every possible type of trombone, although in the Author's opinion, the tone quality of the large bore instruments is a little too light. The alto and medium/large (.525″) trombones are particularly fine instruments. All are very well made and finished; and new, improved instruments continue to appear year by year.

This kind of competition has put other manufacturers in European countries on their mettle, resulting in a general increase in quality control, and greater readiness to respond to the specialized needs of trombonists – all to the benefit of the player.

Care and maintenance

Most professional players are constantly on the look-out for new instruments—new models from the best makers, or new examples of the model which they already use. This does not mean that they are dissatisfied with the instrument which they already have, which is probably well tried and tested, possibly several years old, and regarded as an old friend. But there is always the feeling that the old instrument may be lost or stolen, leaving a gap which could be very difficult to fill. Although the best makes are fairly consistent in their high quality, there are slight variations and professionals prefer to pick their own instrument from a dozen or so similar ones.

When you have found a good trombone for your particular needs, take care of it! So many times one sees during rehearsal intervals, trombones resting on chairs or even on the floor. This seems to me to be particularly foolish—the unwary foot or careless knock can cause havoc with slides and disfigure bell-sections. Modern trombones tend to be made with fairly close tolerances between inner and outer slides. The slightest knock may render a fine instrument useless— perhaps the slide will move, but it will be impossible to play with any kind of artistry, and legato playing in particular will be seriously impaired. I strongly recommend the use of stands or rests for trombones so that they may be properly placed out of harm's way when they are not being used. They are made so that the stand itself supports the bell of the trombone, whilst the slide rests on the floor.

Even if these stands are used, accidental knocking of the end of the slide on music stands or chairs can cause similar damage. Unfortunately the small dents at the end of the slide will affect it when returning to the first position, thus making most of one's playing very difficult. It is really surprising what poor slide action one can become used to. I can hardly over-emphasize the bad effect it can have on one's playing. Any

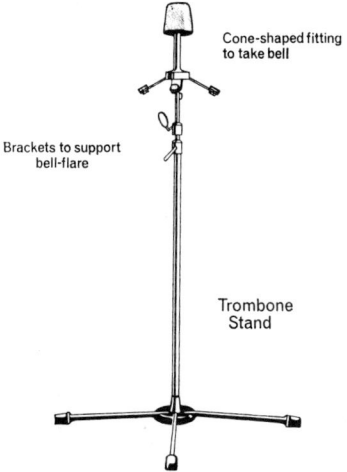

Cone-shaped fitting
to take bell

Brackets to support
bell-flare

Trombone
Stand

small dents must be removed as soon as possible by a competent repairman.

There is an excellent siliconized cream on the market which I strongly recommend for easy slide movement. It has the brand name 'Superslick' and is marketed by C.G. Conn Ltd. One can also use ordinary cold cream. Conn also sell a special oil to be used in minute quantities with 'Superslick'. Only one drop should be used with each application of cream. All creams should be used sparingly and rubbed well into the inner slides, starting at the stocking, where most of it should go. Perhaps just a fraction of this needs to go on the upper end of the inner slide. The inner slide then needs to be sprayed with a fine atomized spray of water. This in combination with the cream forms an excellent lubrication. Although various manufacturers have suggested lubricating oil for slides, every professional player I have met uses cream and water. Oil is messy and much less effective.

New instruments never play as well as old ones in good condition. Almost every new trombone I have played exhibits a kind of rawness and hardness. After a period of use they seem to improve in the way that the owner needs most—the high register becomes more reliable, the low register more full, and so on. The probable explanation of this is that there is a slight molecular movement in the bell, to accommodate the various frequencies that are most used.

One rather extraordinary incident illustrates this very clearly. One of my students had just purchased a new Conn trombone, the model 6H. After he had played the trombone for a week he complained that there was no high D on it. To satisfy my curiosity I took the instrument and played high D about twenty times, at all dynamic levels and eventually as loud as possible. When I handed the instrument back to him, it played high D for him too! Some months after this incident he thanked me for 'putting the D on to his trombone', and said that it had never let him down! While some of this at least may be psychological, these are the facts as they happened, and the settling down of the molecular structure may be a possible explanation.

To overcome the 'newness' of a new trombone, I have heard it suggested that stale milk should be poured through the instrument, in order to coat the inside. This revolting procedure undoubtedly works; but even rinsing with water will have a similar effect. (Personally, I have never found such procedures necessary.)

It is important not to leave trombone slides wet when they are being stored. Electrolytic action can cause corrosion and almost as much wear as ordinary use.

I have often been asked 'should one choose a lacquered or a plated instrument?' Lacquered instruments are usually preferred by professional players in all fields, though at least one authority (Renold Schilke—Chicago) says that properly controlled silver plating is thinner than lacquer and is less likely to affect the characteristics of the instrument. I have one interesting experience in this connexion. My old Conn 8H trombone was relacquered by a London firm (now out of business) which guaranteed that their lacquer was virtually indestructible. So it was. But they forgot to add that it was as thick as two or three coats of paint! The effect was to spoil the playing of the instrument completely. The characteristics which had made this trombone the envy of many professional colleagues—a warm glowing sound in *pp* and *mf* and rich brilliance in *ff*—disappeared, leaving an instrument that could easily be mistaken for an inferior make. After some thought I succeeded in removing the lacquer from just the bell-flare, using a chemical solvent. When cleaned and polished the trombone played better than it had ever done. I then had the recurrent chore of polishing the red-brass bell, but the quality of sound made it worth while. Recent experiments at Boosey & Hawkes indicate that a lacquered finish produces superior tone-quality and easier response than a silver-plated instrument. This is particularly noticeable in best-quality trombones.

As many manufacturers state in their instructions, deposits of food particles, dirt, etc. should never be allowed to build up on a new or old trombone, and everyone should clean out his instrument with warm water, and a flexible brush (obtainable from most dealers—or you can make one with flexible curtain wire and a piece of lint-free rag) every week. The mouthpiece should similarly be brushed out daily.

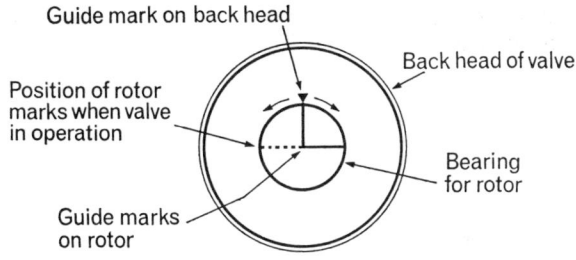

Rotary valves should be cleaned out with recommended manufacturer's lubricant *before* there is any possibility of 'gumming up'. The usual procedure is to clean the moving parts with plenty of oil, dry off any excess oil, then lubricate very sparingly. The guide marks on the back of the valve should be checked. If they are out of alignment (see diagram) the cork or neoprene stops on the front of the valve should be inspected for wear, and if necessary renewed, making sure that the marks now line up. As it is eminently possible for string or cord to break on string valves, the following diagram will show how these should be refitted.

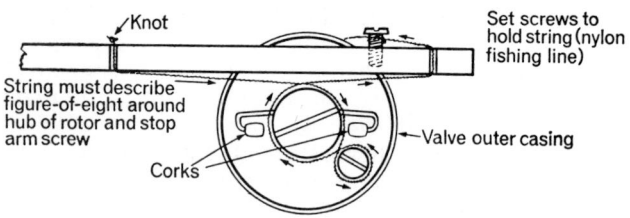

Gig bags

Several manufacturers now produce a soft, padded case as an alternative to the rigid and fairly heavy case which has always been thought necessary to provide adequate protection for the trombone. These so-called 'gig bags' are a boon to commuting trombonists, but need to be handled very carefully since they naturally cannot protect the instrument as well as a conventional fitted case.

POSITIONS AND EMBOUCHURE

Holding the trombone

The trombone is usually held at an angle of about sixty degrees to the vertical. The left hand *must* support the entire weight of the instrument. This may seem very difficult, if not impossible, to the beginner; to him the instrument may seem much too heavy to be held in this way. Most trombones made today are very well balanced, however, and when in a playing position will 'sit' in a perfectly natural and easy way in the left hand. Supporting the weight of the trombone with the right hand will cause premature wear of the outer slide and distort the inner slide, as well as possibly giving rise to bad intonation. In order to hold the instrument more steadily, the index finger of the left hand is extended and presses against the mouthpiece. This considerably improves balance and stability. The player's body should be erect, with the seat well back in the chair. The legs should not be crossed. The whole bodily attitude should be alert and poised, but not tense. The standing position is similar, with shoulders back and head upright.

The slide should be held firmly but lightly by the thumb and index finger of the right hand. Other fingers may support the index finger. The hand and wrist should always be in the same plane, with the elbow doing most of the work. Excessive wrist movement should be avoided (see plates 3–8). This does not mean that the slide action should be at all jerky, but rather that the wrist should not 'flap about', which can create serious problems.

Movement of the slide should be made very *gently*, never too fast, too jerkily or with more force than is necessary. The aim should be fast acceleration but sensitive braking.

Positions

There are seven positions of the trombone slide: the first

position has the slide closed, the fourth position is at the far end of the slide. Here in the last five inches of the inner slide, it expands to a slightly larger diameter to form the 'stocking' which acts as a bearing for the outer slide. The second, third, fifth, and sixth positions are located between the others with no visible indication of exactly where they should be. The distances between the positions become progressively greater, so that there is a difference of about $1\frac{1}{8}$ in. between 1–2 and 6–7. One well known U.S. authority (Mark McDunn) gives the distances between positions as follows:

Positions   Distances

1
    $3\frac{5}{16}$
2
    $3\frac{1}{2}$
3
    $3\frac{11}{16}$
4
    $3\frac{15}{16}$
5
    $4\frac{3}{16}$
6
    $4\frac{7}{16}$
7

These were checked with a stroboscope and apply to the instrument that Mr. McDunn uses. Other makes of trombone may vary slightly, but these are the kinds of measurements that one is likely to find on most trombones.

The embouchure

Sounds on the trombone, as on all brass instruments are made by the regular vibration of air within the instrument. As the player's embouchure, which produces this vibration, is easily the most important part of his equipment, let us consider precisely what happens.

If the lip surfaces are to vibrate, they must be held in a state of controlled tension. To achieve this, it is generally agreed that the lips should be pouted and pursed as in whistling. They are held in a controllable position by a very gentle tensing of muscles surrounding the lips themselves; these muscles pull in the *opposite* direction, i.e. outwards.

As the diagram shows, the muscles surrounding the lips form a very complex structure, which by subtle co-operation allow the lips to vibrate in a controllable manner within the confines of the mouthpiece. The important muscles are the *orbicularis oris*, surrounding the lips themselves, which are subdivided into many muscles which are capable of changing considerably the shape and contours of both upper and lower lips. The muscles which work in conjunction with the orbicularis oris are: the triangularis, which pulls the mouth-corners down and slightly sideways, the platysma which depresses mouth-corners and lowers the jaw (as in yawning), the buccinator, which pulls *back* the mouth-corners, flattens the cheeks, and keeps the lips taut, and the zygomaticus, which *raises* the mouth-corners and draws them to the side (as in smiling and laughing). All this is necessarily involved and complicated to express, and few people outside the medical profession would understand it sufficiently to form a good embouchure: luckily, it is not necessary to be so technical.

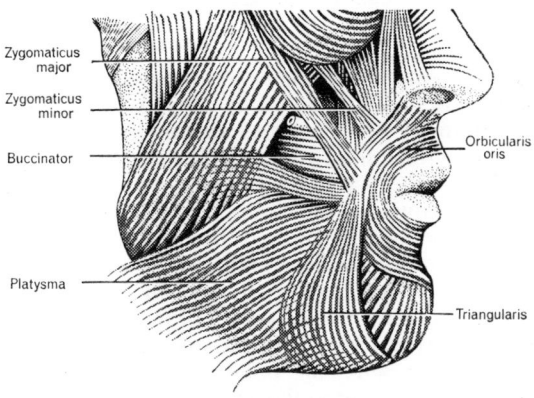

Zygomaticus major
Zygomaticus minor
Buccinator
Platysma
Orbicularis oris
Triangularis

I believe that for an ideal embouchure the easiest, most natural methods should be used. To begin with, the lower jaw should be pushed forward until the teeth are opposite, and arched slightly downwards. With the lips pursed, as in whistling, they are buzzed by pressing them together gently while blowing air between them. The cheeks should not be distended, but allowed to remain in a natural, relaxed position. There should be the merest suggestion of a smile to pull against the pucker.

The characteristic embouchure shape thus described is used by nearly all successful trombone players. A general, although not infallible, guide as to whether these ideas are being followed are the characteristic lines which follow the curve of the upper lip and point downwards on each side of the embouchure. Most trombonists' embouchures show this quite clearly.

The over-riding consideration in the formation of a good embouchure structure is that it must sound good and feel good! The lips and their supporting muscles must feel completely natural and relaxed. The foregoing description sounds somewhat complicated, and may even seem difficult to put into practice to begin with; it is, however, the simplest and easiest and most natural method of forming a good embouchure, which will provide easily a rich, full, 'centred' tone-quality on the trombone.

It has often been erroneously suggested and assumed that the airstream, once it reaches the mouthpiece, goes straight through into the instrument. This can easily be disproved. In the great majority of cases, the air-flow is not, as might be supposed, at right angles to the facial profile, but rather at a downward angle. A hand held out under the chin can easily detect the downward movement of air when the lips are formed into an embouchure and 'buzzed'. (I should add here that there is a very small minority of players of whom the reverse is true; a short upper lip and an undershot jaw may have caused the opposite 'upward' airstream to have been adopted. Very rarely do such players make a success of the trombone. There are just enough of them to prove the exceptions to the rule—the few really fine, mainly jazz players who play this way are to be congratulated upon their very difficult achievement.)

It can be seen quite easily that, as the player moves upwards into the high register of the trombone, he blows more narrowly downwards, eventually playing the highest notes, down almost on to his chin. It can be expressed diagrammatically (see below).

The airstream bounces off the bottom of the mouthpiece cup, finally making a vortex into the bore. Pedal notes are the only ones that seem to go straight into the bore of the mouthpiece. It can readily be seen that the intelligent pointing of the airstream into different parts of the mouthpiece will give, or help to give, a great diversity of range. By altering the shapes of the lip profiles, or, in extreme cases (low register) by pushing out the entire jaw and lower lip, the airflow direction can be changed. In order to facilitate this, I advocate a 'wet' embouchure; I find that this gives greater flexibility than the 'dry' kind and makes sore lips less likely.

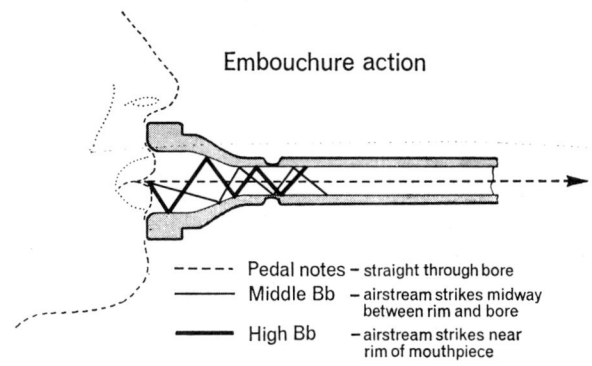

Embouchure action

- - - - Pedal notes – straight through bore
——— Middle Bb – airstream strikes midway
between rim and bore
—— High Bb – airstream strikes near
rim of mouthpiece

This is, of course, by no means the only factor in getting higher or lower notes. As one plays higher, the entire orbicularis oris contracts, rather like a camera lens iris 'stopping down'. The profile of the lower lip also flattens vertically, and the air flowing through the embouchure travels faster. There are several constant, immovable factors; the mouthpiece itself, of course, cannot change; the upper lip remains anchored at its point of contact with the mouthpiece; the corners of the mouth stay exactly as they are. The main movement is in the lower lip and jaw. Although there is a certain amount of movement in the upper lip, this happens within the confines of the mouthpiece. This applies equally to the lower lip, but there is often more activity visible underneath the mouthpiece than above it.

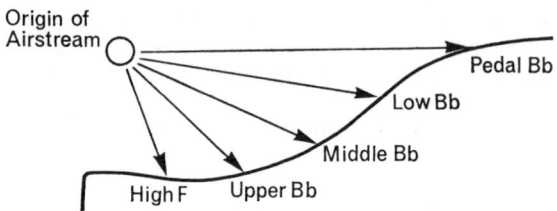

Striking points of airstream on lower section of mouthpiece cup

By protruding the lower lip, arching the chin forward and down, and relaxing the muscular tension within the embouchure it becomes very easy to move into the lower register of the trombone. Here the speed of the flow of air is very much slower, although more air is displaced because the opening in the middle of the embouchure is much wider.

To tell a student to flatten vertically the profile of his lower lip, which is what he will ultimately do as he ascends into the upper reaches of the trombone's range, is rather like suggesting that the moves his smallest toe by itself or rotate his left ear! Whereas it may be possible to do these things in time, given the appropriate exercises, they are not likely to occur spontaneously. In the same way, it is sometimes easier to learn these minute lip movements by moving the lower lip bodily back, as one ascends. This is rather like cracking an egg with a sledge-hammer, and is likely to cause extreme sharpness when playing high, so caution and careful listening are needed; once these tiny muscular lip movements within the lips themselves are working, the lips should be kept parallel, and withdrawal of the lower lip forbidden.

By using the methods outlined above, the trombone can be made to move with comparative ease from the lowest pedal notes to notes four octaves above.

Armed with this knowledge, and having pursed his lips,

pushed forward his jaw, and 'buzzed' into the instrument, the newcomer to the trombone should be able to blow a not particularly refined note in the middle register, perhaps F, B♭, or D. These sounds will soon assume a more 'centred' quality. The presence of a teacher can save many hours of fruitless struggle, as the student becomes accustomed to using muscles which he has never even heard of, much less used before; at this stage as at most others it is absolutely essential to have the best possible professional guidance.

Even with a few weeks' practice behind him, the young player is not likely to have enough command of the subtle movements of the insides of the lips, especially the lower lip, to be able to use his theoretical knowledge of directing the air into different parts of the mouthpiece. Patient practice of slow, gentle slurs, will teach the muscles on the lip to move for him. In the meantime, again under the most careful supervision, the novice should move his lower lip bodily, as described above, taking care not to exaggerate the movements. When the idea of directing the airstream is a reality, he should try to minimize the amount of movement, keeping the lips parallel in an upward movement, and slightly restricting the downward and outward movements. At the same time he should listen continuously for the best sound quality.

The position of the mouthpiece on the mouth is often a cause for concern among students. Most trombone players place the mouthpiece more on the top lip than on the bottom lip—say two-thirds top, one-third bottom. This usually produces the best results. There are, however, some excellent players who reverse these proportions, and who play too well for their mouthpiece placement to be considered wrong. In my own experience, they include players with a brilliant tone-quality, which sometimes appears hard. This is only a tendency, though, and they often more than compensate for it in scintillating technique and 'never miss' high register.

Ideally, given an absolutely regular set of front teeth, the trombonist's embouchure should be exactly in the centre of his mouth. The number of players who have this ideal dental distribution is extremely rare, however, and almost all players play fractionally off-centre, some very much so. It is futile for a teacher to insist on moving a student's mouthpiece position to a more central one, except, of course, when it is wildly wrong, unless his teeth are perfectly regular. One of the penalties for young children beginning the trombone is that their short arm lengths make them tend to pull the instrument round to the right, shifting the mouthpiece to the side of the mouth to reach the 6th and 7th positions. This sort of misplacement should be resisted, either by avoiding 6th and 7th positions, or, more sensibly, by using a B♭ and F trombone. Frank Holton & Co. have a B♭ and G trombone in their student range which serves this purpose admirably.

Given fairly normal teeth and lips, the two-thirds upper, one-third lower system, with the mouthpiece in a central position, should be given preference when starting to play. But it should not be made a definite rule, for there is always an ideal position for the mouthpiece, which, when it has been discovered, produces conspicuously better results in tone-quality, flexibility, and clarity of articulation. The sooner this 'ideal position' is settled in a young player's career, the quicker he is likely to make real progress. Actually it can vary a little from day to day, but not more than about ⅛ in. There is a sensation of inward grip on the mouthpiece which should be actively remembered. The re-creation of these sensations on the lips is, after all, the object of practice, and for this reason progress can be quite fast in the early stages of playing. This presumes a good teacher and regular practice.

There is a natural tendency for beginners to press too hard on the mouthpiece. Before the vibrating and support muscles have been properly formed it is quite usual and natural for this pressure to cause a rather sore-looking red ring. Most professional trombone players will use far more pressure than this on occasion—at the end of a concert, at least. They have had many years to build up a really powerful muscular structure, capable of taking more punishment than that of the beginner. Despite this, however, the best results are never accomplished with heavy mouthpiece pressure, and for 95 per cent of the time even the toughest professional uses little more than minimum pressure needed for an air-seal.

By practising on the mouthpiece alone (see p.28) it is possible to develop enough embouchure strength to solve the problem. Excessive mouthpiece pressure will effectively prevent progress, by reducing or cutting off the blood circulation of the lips, which like every other part of the body need sustaining with oxygen. Prolonged heavy mouthpiece pressure will bruise the comparatively delicate tissue and cause swelling. Some swelling is, as we have seen, inevitable in a beginner. The most usual problem in my experience is the combination of heavy pressure with a stretched top-lip embouchure. As this seems to occur with depressing regularity among young trombonists, I think it is worth discussion under a separate heading.

One of the most frequent problems that I have met in young students who have been studying for some years without making much headway, is that of stretched lips. Here the top lip, particularly, is stretched by the action of the 'smile' muscles—zygomatic major and buccinator—not pursed as suggested earlier. When the lips are stretched in this way, not only do they become thinner in texture, but the embouchure itself takes on a flatter contour, oval rather than round. This gives a much harder, thinner sound quality, very restricted in volume and range. In order to hold the lips in shape as the player ascends, he has to press harder upon the mouthpiece. This is sometimes called the 'smile-and-press' embouchure.

It is well known that the only positive function of any muscle in the entire body is to contract. When a muscle contracts it becomes more dense and thus stronger. If the lips are stretched, they are conversely weakened. Although, as we have seen, successful trombonists limit the pressure of the mouthpiece, there is still enough to bring a stretched-lip embouchure to a state of semi-paralysis after even a short playing session. This is only one of the many problems that come from a stretched embouchure: suffice it to say that I have never yet met a really successful trombonist who used this method. I confidently never expect to do so!

Physical characteristics needed by a trombone player

Some of these are fairly obvious, others not so. Here are some suggestions.

(1) Arms of at least average length
(2) A top lip which is long vertically

    (3) Regular largish front teeth
    (4) A high roof to the mouth
    (5) A reasonable lung capacity

One should add—a perceptive ear, good natural rhythm, a sense of purpose, and great industriousness. I do not recommend that a child of less than about twelve years of age should be taught the trombone. A certain degree of maturity of body—lip and arm length—and mind are necessary.

It is important, and becomes increasingly so as a players's career develops, that he takes good care of his completely unique and irreplaceable equipment—his embouchure. Regular visits to the dentist are absolutely essential. A sympathetic dentist is worth seeking out. A trombonist's dental problems are not really different from anyone else's, but they may cause a complete breakdown in his playing ability, in the case of a damaged front tooth for example. Regular dental and oral hygiene are, of course, essential. The lips are really very delicate and carefully adjusted complex muscular structures. Even the slightest bruising or injury can cause disturbances that may take days or weeks of careful remedial practice to put right. It has always seemed to me that changes in mouthpiece rim-shape, however small, can cause the biggest problems. I have heard unbelievably bad playing from some of the world's finest brass players when too injudicious experimentation with the mouthpiece had upset the delicate muscular balance of the lips. For this reason, it is extremely unwise to try other mouthpieces or instruments too close to a performance, and this is why it is most unusual for brass to double on woodwind or other brass. I have even heard it said that a really passionate kiss can spoil a trombonist's embouchure for several hours!

3
BASIC PROCEDURES

'Warm-up' procedures and practice methods

More than is generally realized, playing any brass instrument for an extended period at a high standard is very much an athletic pursuit. It demands prolonged concentration, precise co-ordination of all the faculties, and a good physical condition. While these prerequisites are improved by study and exercise, the trombonist needs, as much as any other athlete, to train seriously in order to improve his performance.

Just as the 100-yard specialist needs to start his day's training with a gradual limbering up—he would not dream of timing his sprint until he had had a 'work-out' of at least 40–60 minutes—so the trombonist too needs a very gradual warm-up. There are so many young players, particularly gifted ones, who will open the case, assemble the instrument, and see whether they can still play altissimo F as well as yesterday! This is just as crazy as expecting the 100-yard sprinter to perform from 'cold'. I would even go so far as to say that a player who has to perform for any length of time needs to warm up for at least 20 minutes—possibly even more. Any short-cuts will seriously impair his ability to stay the distance. That first high F will probably cost an hour's playing later in the day.

To begin with, the muscles of the embouchure should be gently stimulated by playing a few notes on the mouthpiece alone. This 'buzzing' as a preparatory exercise can save valuable time; when the warm-up proper starts, on the assembled instrument, the first sounds appear much more easily. These should be the most easily and gently blown notes—middle F or low Bb separated with rests equal in length to each note. Once the embouchure is functioning well, these long notes should be played in adjacent pairs, with, say, 8 beats on each note. This ensures controlled production and clear note endings. After another rest, slow, low slurs should be played, again using just two notes at a time. The next step is to speed up this procedure slightly, going on to more complex patterns of lip slurs, on 2, 3, or 4 notes. After another short break this may be carried into the upper register. The guiding principle behind all this is that nothing too difficult or straining should be tried too soon.

This 15 or 20 minute warm-up procedure is already available in published form—in the *Warm-Up Exercises* by Emory Remington (Pyraminx Publications [Robert King Music Co.]).

When the warm-up is completed the student may continue his practice. He should organize this very carefully, progressing from scales, arpeggios, and lip flexibility exercises, to studies on specific aspects of technique. More specialized work, such as high note practice, which is usually very arduous, should be left until the very end of the practice period.

It is even more necessary for the professional player to warm up properly. I have found from bitter experience that the kind of warm-up outlined above is absolutely necessary if one is to play, say, two or three heavy recording sessions in a day, or a long rehearsal in the morning for a concert in the evening. The temptation to try out the difficult bits should be resisted. There is much sense in the often heard band-room remark that 'It's too late now!' For if the rehearsal has been done properly, with the right amount of concentration, the performance will take care of itself.

Most professional players neglect regular practice when they are playing really well. Who can blame them, when in most branches of the profession they already have to work very long hours anyway? When, of necessity, they begin to practise really hard, because their playing has slipped below its usual standard, improving their technique can be a most difficult and arduous task. The remedy is, I believe, to practise when one is playing really well, when everything seems so easy that one cannot remember or imagine a bad performance. It is *now* that progress can be made. The depressingly bad performance, when one cannot remember a good one, is probably a sign that a break is needed from the instrument.

Every trombonist, whether a student or professional, needs to take a holiday away from the instrument every year or so. After three weeks' relaxation or concentration on something else, one's 'playing-in'—the careful practice needed before resuming normal playing activities—has to be carefully thought-out. If a daily warm-up was essential, this playing-in is even more so. Years have been spent in the gradual building of sound quality and technique, and no risks should be taken by forcing one's playing back to its pre-holiday standard by premature enthusiasm.

The first day back at the instrument should consist simply of a 15-minute warm-up. On the second day there should probably be two separate 20-minute spells, at least 8 hours apart. By the third day more extensive practice may be undertaken, possibly in two 30-minute sessions. After these 3 days one's playing should have almost returned to normal, and a good hour's practice at each end of the day will reveal that the time spent away from the instrument has been of enormous benefit: one's tone will be full and rich, and one's technique really well established again. It is as well to try and avoid work which calls for continuous use of the high register, or very long hours of heavy playing, before the necessary stamina has been built up—and this usually takes a further week or two.

Breathing is the aspect of playing that seems to suffer most after a long break; some walking and deep breathing exercises of the kind mentioned on p.36 will undoubtedly help.

Frequent breaks are essential when practising; after a 20-minute warm-up have a 10-minute break, then half and hour's practice followed by a half-hour break, then another half-hour's practice and so on. Most students simply do not practise enough. It has been wisely said that 'practice time is like money in the bank'. While working professionally the player may be so heavily committed as regards time and physical endurance that he may not have enough of either to practise very much. But at some stage in every player's career he must devote five or six hours a day to careful practice for perhaps six months or a year. Such an investment of time is essential during one's student years as it enables the young player to make do for months or even years with as little as an hour's practice per day.

I am *in general* against the idea of practising the repertoire and individual difficult passages to excess. It is much better to work on the specific technical requirement of any particular passage—the piece will then take care of itself. Of course, the difficult solos in the orchestral, concerto, and sonata repertoire need to be worked on, but not to the exclusion of everything else.

One suggestion which I have always found useful is that one's private practice for a definite occasion should be spaced out carefully *before* the appointed day. If one has something really demanding and difficult—i.e. a concerto or solo appearance on a Friday for example—then most of one's practice should have been completed on the preceding Wednesday and Monday. This certainly applies to an orchestral player who normally takes his daily work very much in his stride, and who occasionally takes on what is for him an unaccustomed role as a soloist. When such an important occasion arises care should be taken to rest the lip for 6–8 hours before the solo appearance, apart from a gentle warm-up half an hour before the actual concerto or solo piece.

Mouthpiece practice

The idea of practising on the mouthpiece alone is an American one of comparatively recent origin and is well worth copying. Many trombonists play in somewhat inefficient ways and often tend to 'buzz' with the embouchure a slightly different pitch from the one which the slide position would give. It is very revealing to remove the mouthpiece and try to play on it the exact notes of a study or exercise. Usually the sounds produced are very inaccurate in pitch and normally it is only the instrument itself that shapes these unpromising beginnings into the right pitches. This gives the resulting notes a poor quality. By practising the *exact* pitches on the mouthpiece, the 'centring' of the sounds on the instrument can be very much improved.

This method of mouthpiece practice can also reveal poor articulation and embouchure control and even tone deficiencies. I strongly recommend this type of practice to my students, but insist on two points being observed throughout:

(1) Play on the mouthpiece *exactly* as you play on the instrument; do not adopt a different 'feel' or method, just because it appears to work better.

(2) Frequently check intonation with a piano or with the trombone.

If, as sometimes occurs, it is found that there is hardly any control of the sound on the mouthpiece to begin with, then perhaps the simulation of the resistance that the instrument itself gives, by putting the little finger partially over the end of the mouthpiece, will help the embouchure to respond.

Every kind of study—long notes, scales, slurring exercises—can be used for this kind of practice. Sometimes when a passage with awkward intervals presents more than usual difficulty, practice with just the mouthpiece can correct it, so that when the instrument is reassembled the offending passage becomes apparently easy.

Production

The clarity and precision with which a really fine trombonist begins his notes is often a cause of admiration, particularly from the less skilled. A good production, like any other facet of one's technique, needs careful and continuous working on but it can be acquired without too much difficulty. The acquisition of a clean production will open the gateway to unimagined technical ability, and make it possible to acquire a really polished orchestral or solo style.

We all know that the tongue is used to start the sound, usually with the enunciation of the syllable 'too!' or 'doo!' What is generally not understood, even by some professional players, is that the tongue-action is frequently over-emphasized and results in an unpleasantly explosive start to loud notes, or an unpredictable faltering 'te-her' beginning to soft notes. In considering this over-emphasis let us therefore discuss the exact function of the tongue.

In order to provide sounds precisely when required the flow of air between the lips has to be regulated. The diaphragm, the dome-shaped muscular structure below the lungs, helps the lungs to push air through to the vibrating lips, rather like the handles of a pair of bellows. By a swift withdrawing movement the tongue suddenly releases the air, which energizes the embouchure. This withdrawing movement has to be carefully synchronized with the upward thrust of the diaphragm; when this is well done the embouchure should vibrate instantaneously. If on the other hand these actions are not synchronized, or there is not enough push from the diaphragm to give breath support—or especially where the embouchure itself is not properly co-ordinated—then the result is anything but good.

Whenever a student complains that his tone production is faulty and finds difficulty in putting it right, I ask him to play me an easy note—a middle Bb for instance—but with *no tongue*. Usually nothing happens! A fuzzy half-hearted note may perhaps come out fractionally later. If the tongue is deliberately omitted from his practice for a few days—not just for long notes, but for all of them—and the student is made to play simply by pushing air through the embouchure with the aid of the diaphragm, he very soon discovers how the embouchure should work. The next step is to discover the best point of contact for the tongue; but before this is done another basic principle has to be learned. The process of starting a note begins with inhaling and continues as the air moves out continuously without stopping or becoming 'bottled up' behind the tongue. A momentary tongue-tied hesitation will prevent any kind of controlled production from taking place, for the pent-up air will rush out in a completely uncontrolled way. It follows then that the tongue has to be placed in a position only a split second before the note starts. He who hesitates is lost!

The placing of the tongue during the split second when the inhaled air changes direction is the next point to be considered. Despite the speed of its actions the tongue must make a completely airtight seal, or the production will not start cleanly.

The position of the tongue alters slightly from register to register, because the shape of the mouth changes when playing high or low. Thus the point at which the air-seal can be made will vary from high up behind the gums for the upper register, to low down behind the teeth, or even on the top lip, for the lowest register. The part of the tongue that makes this sealing contact is slightly more than the tip, and the semicircular shape should make a good fit with the rim section which it momentarily touches.

If the student remains at all unconvinced about the importance of not holding back the air behind the tongue, he should deliberately 'bottle' (i.e. hold back), and will feel the muscular tension that has built up on his throat and neck muscles and the muscles around the embouchure. Even trying to speak under such conditions is difficult! It is obviously impossible to make one's production relaxed and controlled until this fault is corrected.

The next step for the student is to remove the risks of imprecise attack, cracked notes, or uneven playing in general through a not completely dependable method of production. As we have seen, tongue position will vary with register, and also with legato and semilegato articulations. But apart from these variations, the student's aim must be to see that the action and pressure of the tongue remain the same, on any given note, whatever the dynamic accent or length of the note. To give an example: middle F whether

played   𝅗𝅥   or   ♩   or   𝅗𝅥.   or   𝅜   or   ♪
       ff   *fp*   *mp >*   *fp*   *p*

should always have the same tongue placing. The diaphragm has enough power to take care of the accents; the embouchure and the glottis can usefully open up for the *ff* and close down for the *pp*. Although these techniques are very difficult for the player who has been exhorted in the past to 'tongue harder', they make it possible for every player to possess a perfect and precise production dependably in all registers. After all, what happens to the notes if one tongues harder? Nothing! The tongue merely presses harder before the note starts, bottles the air, and transfers to itself the functions of the diaphragm. It would help the average student to understand these processes if the word 'attack' were dropped in describing the production of sounds—'release' would describe more accurately what actually happens.

Proper control of the diaphragm and the glottis is also very important to the security and continuity of the notes whose actual production we have described so far. Breath support is also of enormous importance, and the position of the diaphragm has a great influence on the stability of the note in progress. Broadly speaking, the diaphragm rises and stays raised in the high register, and tends to tighten in a lower position in the lower register. The two basic features are that in the upper register the air flows quickly through a small aperture while in the lower the reverse is true.

The position of the tongue after the note has started is of paramount importance. For the upper register, not only is the tongue sealing-point high, but its position remains high in the mouth for the duration of the note; it helps the air to move faster, as I have just described. For the lower register the tongue is much lower in the mouth and stays in suspended animation, as the thicker, slowly-moving column of air moves out. The same idea applies in whistling, as a few moments experimenting will show.

The glottis, which exists primarily to help speech, can be used advantageously in trombone playing also, by acting as a valve which cuts down even further to air passing to the embouchure. With the glottis just opened, a really well-controlled pp can be produced effortlessly; fully open, the loudest short ff chord. It is also used to terminate notes, and that is the next subject to be considered.

It is simple, one would think, to end a note—just do not allow any more air from the lungs into the instrument. Unfortunately there is no way of stopping the air, unless one runs out of breath or puts something in the way of the airstream, like shutting off a tap. One most unpleasant and unmusical way of doing this is to stop the end of the note by replacing the tongue in the production position—or more likely between the teeth. I needly hardly add that although this fault—for fault it is—persists in some untrained or badly trained players, it is one of the worst with which any brass instrumentalist can be afflicted. If it was wrong to bottle up the air before the note starts, then it is more incorrect to bottle it after the note has finished! In practice this habit usually amounts to a kind of pre-selection of the next note and has to be eradicated before any progress can be made.

The correct way to end notes is simply by closing the glottis. A great many trombonists when confronted with this fact start by trying to do something extraordinary and complicated with the throat. In point of fact simple vocal experiments—such as saying 'aah!' and then closing the glottis to prevent any more air coming out while the mouth is still open—should be enough to convince the student that what he is doing is perfectly natural and easy. The most pleasant way of ending even short notes is with a tiny diminuendo, and this can be accomplished very easily by closing the glottis a little more gradually, simultaneously relaxing the presence of air from the diaphragm.

Breathing

Others have written at great length about the finer anatomical points of breathing and breath control. I would like however to make a few observations on this particular topic as it relates to the trombonist, and in the light of my own experience.

Ordinary breathing bears little resemblance to what is required of a successful trombonist. Most people only breathe properly in conditions of extreme physical endeavour. To be successful the trombonist must learn to do this as a matter of course.

The lungs are capable of taking in far more air than is generally supposed. In order to fill them completely and quickly the throat must be fully open and relaxed. The lungs, like a milk jug, must fill from the bottom first. To accomplish this, the diaphragm should be pushed forward and down. In this position there is enough room for the lungs to expand fully—they should also fill out sideways as well as downwards. To inhale properly through the corners of the mouth, with the mouthpiece in the playing position, the diaphragm movement should therefore be made first so that the lower lung-span can fill, and then the upper part of the lungs last. This sounds complicated, but it should all happen in one continuous movement. The body and trunk should be upright and not slouching in any way. Although breathing exercises are usually practised slowly, deep *fast* breathing is essential for practical purposes—complete inflation of the lungs should be achieved within the space of a crotchet beat in Allegro tempo.

This is, of course, only part of the story, although it is the part most often neglected. Exhaling is an equally important aspect. For inhalation the diaphragm is relaxed, but to exhale it resumes its dome-like shape, or tries to, and in doing so propels the air from the lungs.

The importance of the speed of the air-flow in relation to playing low or high cannot be over-emphasized. The low register in general needs a slower speed at a greater volume—a high amperage at a lower voltage—to use electrical terms. Conversely the upper range demands a greater velocity but with a smaller volume of air—a high voltage–lower amperage relationship.

Efficient breathing is probably the most continuing concern of the professional player. Even when all his other problems have long been mastered, correct breathing needs careful concentration; if it is at all neglected it may result in otherwise inexplicable mistakes which may not appear to be related to breathing problems.

The actual position of the diaphragm while playing is also of great importance. In the lower register it needs to be somewhat extended, forward and low, and it gradually comes up and in, as the player moves into the upper reaches of the trombone range. In the altissimo register it must feel tight and high for security. These facts offer easy solutions of what are well-known difficulties in movements from low to high registers. This passage in Richard Strauss's *Also Sprach Zarathustra* is an interesting example.

The high D taken alone can be played without any more than ordinary difficulty. But played as part of a *ff* passage begun on low A, which reaches up to middle D before shooting up another octave, legato, this becomes very difficult indeed for many players. By holding the diaphragm artificially high throughout the entire passage, the high D almost literally falls out of the instrument!

The main breathing problem that I meet in trombone students is the ignorance of the fact that correct breathing is largely a matter of taking enough air in, or of remembering to make a big enough effort to do so, without disturbing the rest of the playing functions. If this problem is never tackled seriously the student is unlikely ever to develop the necessary lung capacity or strength in the muscular structure of the diaphragm.

Conversely, the conscientious student may try too hard and take more breath than he actually needs. Whereas this is unlikely to happen on the bass trombone or tuba, the upper register of the trombone needs less air, and 'over-breathing'—the need to rid the lungs of excess air at the end of a phrase—may occur. This is to be preferred, however, to being completely out of breath at the end of a phrase. The terrifying lack of control which results at the end of a sustained soft passage when this happens is caused by there being no air left for the diaphragm to push, in order to exert its steadying influence. It is better to take an extra breath in a not-too-obvious place than to risk this happening.

(A minor point, but one which is often encountered, is that playing immediately after a heavy meal, with too tight a waistband, can often restrict one's breathing and breath capacity, possibly just enough to wreck carefully organized breathing plans.)

Playing any brass instrument professionally is as much an athletic as an intellectual occupation. The first time that one plays after a holiday brings this home very clearly! Even if care has been taken to make sure that embouchure and tongue are working satisfactorily one always feels short-winded for a day or two. Regular exercise of a not necessarily strenuous nature is the best way to combat this problem whenever it occurs.

I am often asked by students how they might improve their

lung capacity. Apart from regular practice of long notes, with plenty of crescendo–diminuendo, the consciousness of the need to breathe deeply can also help. It has even been suggested, quite rightly, in my opinion, that it is better to try to increase the lung capacity *away* from the instrument. While walking at a steady speed, the breath should be inhaled over six or seven paces, and exhaled over a similar time. Both inhalation and exhalation can be increased by one or two paces until the improvement has doubled or trebled the available lung capacity.

4
TECHNICAL SKILLS

Intonation

The trombone has been described as the only perfect wind instrument. This somewhat extravagant claim refers to its capacity for perfect intonation by means of the infinitely variable tube length of its slide. By the same token, if it can produce the best intonation, in unskilled hands it can produce the worst.

In common with every other brass instrument, the trombone is able to play the notes of the harmonic series on its basic tube length without moving the slide at all.

The 7th and 11th harmonies, which on the Bb trombone appear as Ab and high Eb, are considerably flat and sharp respectively; too much so to be used in the 1st position.

As with every brass instrument some of the remaining notes tend to be flatter and some sharper than the notes of, say, the piano, which uses the equally-tempered scale. Modern instrumental design and construction tend to reduce these pitch variations to a minimum, and the careful selection and fitting of a mouthpiece can also help the problem. However it is really the careful, albeit unconscious, collaboration of ear and lip structure which is the main factor in correcting the small deviations in intonation. The following diagram shows notes which most often tend to be either too sharp or too flat:

Although it is absolutely essential for slide positions to be 'corrected' for those harmonies which are too sharp or too flat, many student tend to 'over correct' and this dangerous tendency must be carefully watched.

Players using a stretched upper lip will probably find that they will play all the notes in the upper register too sharp—theirs is a special problem (see p.105) and the advice of a good teacher should be sought. Even when there is no basic embouchure problem, the same fault—sharpness in the extreme high register (from Bb upwards) may still be evident. I have experienced this with some students who have developed habits of excess pressure and 'stretch' because their ear dictates a higher pitch than the instrument would provide. Instinctive stretch/press reactions are brought about by the collaboration of the ear and lip muscles. Any increase to extremely loud dynamic levels will intensify this problem. Here again this is very difficult to solve without a sympathetic teacher, who can ensure that his student's equipment will not hinder him. Extremes of fortissimo playing in orchestra or band can sometimes cause high trombone parts to be played too sharp, but may have the reverse effect in the low and middle register, when flatness may be caused when the player tries to displace too much air, with his embouchure too open, in an effort to make a bigger sound—here compromise seems the answer—most of us prefer loud playing to be in tune!

The principle on which the trombone is based, that of the extending slide increasing the overall tube length, thus providing different complete harmonic series, works on proportional rather than fixed tube lengths. Each successively lower position is a little longer, although it still makes a difference of only a semitone. It follows then, that any differences in intonation in the 1st position become magnified and therefore more easily distinguished in the extreme positions. This is a useful fact to bear in mind when trying out a new instrument and one which needs to be borne in mind when using long alternative positions.

The overtone structure—i.e. the harmonic series—which is present on every note, can be a useful guide to really fine intonation. The quality of the trombone section which, I think, is one of the most beautiful sounds in the whole of musical experience, depends for its grandeur on the just-heard blending of overtones, octaves higher than the played notes. It is no exaggeration to describe these sounds as a 'heavenly choir' about the written sounds. In practice, these overtones blend well with upper horn and trumpet notes and high woodwind and strings filling out the whole spectrum of colour. This only happens when the intonation is perfect, providing the reward for all the many hours of slow, careful practice of scales and intervals which is the only way to build up a really dependable sense of intonation.

Although in theory the trombonist must listen really carefully to every note in each position, as he plays, in order to check the intonation minutely, this is regrettably not possible all the time when playing in orchestra or band. There are so many other thought-processes to cope with—reading, interpretation, following the conductor and one's colleagues—that one must rely on muscular memory to learn to play habitually in the exact positions. The term muscular memory may be more readily understood if expressed in more homely terms. There are many muscular movements in everyday life that are undertaken without any thought, certainly without looking. Reaching for the kitchen door-handle, changing gear in a car, tying one's shoelaces, for example. Playing the trombone is more complex and involved than any of these activities, but the same processes, those of unconscious but precise and definite movements, are used.

This really is one of the secrets of being a really good trombonist: one's muscular movements and reactions should be so well practised that they can be depended upon completely, and become instinctive—'second-nature'. Accurate slide-positioning, then, must depend primarily upon muscular memory, evolved from intensive practice of scales and long notes, cross-checking with the same note in more than one position, bearing in mind the tendencies pointed out in the diagram on page 37.

Problems of intonation vary tremendously depending upon whether a trombonist is playing by himself, in a trombone quartet, as the only trombone in a brass quintet or orchestra, or in a trombone section in band or orchestra. Trombones alone or in groups of trombones can produce really perfect intonation. It is obviously not possible to play the trombone only in these circumstances, and the trouble usually begins when other instruments join the trombones, and when their intonation is perhaps less able to be altered. Before he knows it, the capable and musicianly trombonist has accommodated his colleagues' intonation problems, but may have created some for himself in disturbing his 'muscular memory' structure. Left to themselves, a quartet of trombones will tend to produce a beautiful, untempered intonation, comparable to that of a string quartet. Ensemble playing is, of course, absolutely essential for a student and a group of just three or four trombones can provide the utmost benefit.

In the symphony orchestra, careful seating arrangements can minimize problems which are otherwise endemic. If the first trombone sits behind the first trumpet and is jammed up against the timpani this is virtually guaranteed to destroy any possibilities of good intonation and intelligent musical co-operation. The trumpet player has then to adapt his tuning to the first trombone instead of vice-versa; and the trombonist, because of his proximity to the timpani, probably cannot hear what he himself is doing. Yet this is regarded as a standard seating arrangement by many symphony orchestras! It is now coming to be realized that the first trumpet should sit next to the first trombone, just as the first flute and first oboe, or the first clarinet and the first bassoon sit together. If this is not practicable, then one section should not play directly into the ears of the other! Perhaps the removal of the timpani from the sacred centre spot, which many conductors prefer because of the spectacular effect, would help to solve these problems.

It has always been my personal preference to sit on the right of my own section. In this position the first trombonist can really influence the playing of his section. Perhaps the modern instruments which we use, with eight-inch or nine-inch bells, have something to do with this, but many experiments involving sitting the other way have proved to me that it is distinctly less successful. The second and third players simply cannot hear well enough what the first player does, thus wrecking any attempts at sectional nuances and phrasing.

Even worse than the seating I have described, with trombones blowing down the necks of trumpet players, is the much dreaded horns-in-front-of-trombones-arrangement. Both horn players and trombonists alike agree that any attempt to play louder than mezzo-piano is certain to cause complete lack of control—split notes by the dozen—and finally actual physical discomfort in the embouchure. Each player can feel on his lips the effect of his colleagues' playing.

Bass trombonists often have a particular problem, since they may have to try to stay in tune with the tuba players, whose intonation is less able to be corrected. The general high standard of tuba playing, however, makes this much less of a problem than it used to be.

An important point in considering sectional intonation is one of balance. What is often suspected to be faulty intonation may, on closer consideration, turn out to be simply a question of one or more parts being louder or (more usually) softer than the others. It is especially important for the larger-bored bass trombone not to dominate, particularly in the middle register.

Only on rare occasions can we find concert halls where conditions of temperature and humidity are ideal. The trombonist has to make sure that his instrument is warm enough during the performance, even if he has had to wait for perhaps half an hour before playing. Simply breathing gently through it should accomplish this; failure to do so will result in a slightly flatter pitch, since sound waves travel a little more slowly in the cold air within the instrument.

Speed and precision in slide action

Probably the most fascinating aspect of the trombone from the audience's point of view is to see a player or section of players tackling with gusto fast music which involves energetic slide movement. Although this presents the least of his difficulties to the accomplished player, it certainly looks and sometimes sounds hard!

In the chapter on holding the trombone, we saw that the right-hand wrist is kept more or less straight, to cut down too many unpredictable joint-movements. In making a slide movement the first problem to be overcome is the inertia of the slide. It needs quite a firm push, outwards with the thumb or inwards with the index finger. On the way down, the index and the third finger act as a brake, while the thumb brakes upward movements. This may sound very straightforward, but unfortunately the natural result of these movements is that the hand travels not in a straight line but in an arc. Just as the violinist compensates for this by turning his wrist, the trombonist slightly projects his shoulder for 5th, 6th, and 7th positions.

The actual slide movements should in both theory and practice take up as little time as possible, whether one is playing long or short notes. Perfect co-ordination of breath control, tongue-action, and slide movement are absolutely essential. Having been told all this, young players often find that in a valiant effort to move the slide as quickly as possible they jerk it, so that the embouchure becomes disturbed—even battered—by the violence of the movement. I should add that a slick fast slide action has to be carefully studied—a quick acceleration from rest, and a controlled 'cushioned' braking to stop. None of this should be obtrusive, and any great effort to make it happen must not be noticeable. In fact 'effortless' seems a good word to describe how this should appear. The right hand should hold the slide firmly but gently, with just two fingers and thumb.

One particular problem here is often the moving back of the slide to first position. Only careful practice (with the thumb 'brake') will prevent the slide from either stopping short or crashing against the stops with distinctly unpleasant effects on the embouchure.

Some players use a definite wrist action to return from 7th to 6th or 5th positions and vice-versa. This is not necessarily the best method but it is quite a good idea, and is probably neater than involving the whole arm. The only condition that I place upon its use is consistency. The pattern of joint movements has to be learned and always used in precisely the same way; players with comparatively short arms will probably have to support the slide with the 2nd and 3rd fingers in the 7th position.

One important aspect of trombone technique that is often overlooked is the fact that however short the notes in running passages may be, they do still have a definite duration. The old-fashioned concept of a continuously moving slide is no doubt graceful to look at, but certainly guarantees that some notes are played out of tune. The slide must stay in the correct position for the duration of the note, however short it may be. This idea will often give rise to the somewhat odd effect in fast passages that the slide appears to click into place, to 'slot' into each position. It should certainly appear to do this, but in a very controlled way, so as not to jerk the instrument at each movement. If the acceleration and braking are practised thoroughly then the slide action need never be a barrier to the acquisition of a really fine technique.

The acquisition of a fast tongue

The ability to rattle off passages is usually very much admired, perhaps more so on the trombone than on other brass instruments. After all, trombonists have the relatively clumsy slide to contend with, rather than the agile piston valves, which with a tiny finger-tip movement can alter the length of the tube at the player's will.

There are, however, problems of tonguing speeds which have to be tackled exactly as on any other brass instrument.

In the section on 'Production' we saw how the tongue makes a completely hermetic air-seal for the split second before the note starts. This applies to the playing of semibreves just as it does to semiquavers. The beginner should perfect the 'clean' start to all notes, before attempting to speed up tonguing processes. Fast tonguing should never be at the expense of clarity. At a certain speed, which varies between 400 and 520

per minute ($\eighthnote$ s, when $\quarternote = 100-130$) most players have a

natural 'blank' spot at which they find it difficult to play rhythmically and clearly. At a faster speed the tongue appears to free itself, and will 'run' freely. The actual speed of fastest tonguing is very variable, and often overlaps the speed at which double-tonguing may be used. Before considering multiple tonguing let us first investigate the phenomena described above.

When the tongue 'bounces' in a natural way it still makes the same clean seal that it makes for single notes. It does so in a very light way and only *just* seals, so that the airstream is only momentarily broken. This approximates to the dreaded 'stopping with the tongue' that we all so strenuously avoid, the difference being that the lightness of the tongue-seal and the neat co-ordination of its action with the continuously support-ing breath makes a stream of identical notes.

The speed limitations, or blank spots, mentioned above, are related, assuming that everything is being done correctly, to one's nervous system rather than to the technique outlined above. Running downstairs or saying tongue-twisters will present similar problems—the body finds them very difficult at certain speeds. Violinists have exactly the same problems in playing spiccato. I have found that the only remedy is to practise carefully the difficult passage, starting at a speed just slower than the one found awkward, always checking with a metronome. This enables the tongue to work freely without building up those tensions in the lower part of the embouchure and neck, that actively prevent the tongue from moving naturally. It is thus possible to build up the 'slow' speed of free tongue movement and to slow down the slightly less controlled 'bounce' action.

I would always recommend this acquisition of a really fast and controllable single-tongue speed range as far more positive and can be louder than double or triple tonguing, and is much more effective in an orchestral tutti.

Double and triple tonguing

By momentarily closing the mouth with the back of the tongue and saying 'kah' the airstream can be broken without using the front part of the tongue. Thus rested, the tip of the tongue can alternate with the back, and by combining the two, alternately, with the syllables'T–K–T–K' a clean, clear, even staccato can result, at speeds impossible to match with a single tonguing. The enunciation of a clear 'kah' sound may first present some problems, and is unlikely at first to match the clarity of the 'tah'. But diligent practice of the 'K' articulation alone—it is a fairly quick movement—followed by very slow crotchet T–K—will improve this. The student must emphatically *not* move on to faster speeds, however tempted he may be, until the sounds and articulations are perfectly matched in every detail.

It should be realized that the principles described above—of a complete hermetic air-seal for the split second before the note starts— apply as much to double as to single tonguing.

Triple tonguing is to be studied in the same way, and the speed of the eventual triplets is limited only by the T's which come together in either of the suggested groupings—TTK TTK or TKT TKT. Triple tonguing is often a feature of band-solos, where a single triplet on each note of the tune can be found as a 'variation'. In music of this kind, it is absolutely essential to be able to triple tongue fluently. Once again, practice should begin very, very slowly, with evenness of articulation and of sound the primary requirement. Speed comes much later, and can be achieved simply be careful practice. Often in the symphony orchestra, or in other groups for that matter, where quick triplets rather than the 'triple-tonguing polka' effect is required, some players prefer to use an alternating TKT KTK TKT, which, assuming they are *absolutely* even, can be accented with a slight diaphragm push on the first note of each '3'. This effect is perfectly permissible, and can be clearer and stronger than the usual triple-tonguing pattern.

Scales

All scales, major and minor, covering the entire available compass of the trombone must be learned really thoroughly. It is not enough to read through them occasionally or, as frequently happens with young students, to 'rattle' off the major scales in flat keys at the expense of the more rarely used sharp and minor keys. The more distant sharp keys usually present greater difficulties of intonation. E major and B minor for instance are notoriously difficult. I have often noticed that young trombonists—or even older ones who have played only in bands—have never played in any keys sharper than G major or E minor. Even professional players find that most of their intonation problems come in the extreme, least used, sharp keys. Although these remarks may seem somewhat platitudinous they really apply to the trombone even more than to instruments which have more facile ways of playing in different keys. It is absolutely essential to persevere with slow, careful scale practice in *all* keys, until they reach such a state of perfection that playing in any key becomes completely instinctive.

The main benefit to be derived from this kind of practice, apart from the obvious improvements to intonation, is the inevitable speeding up of the thought-processes and muscular reactions associated with sight-reading. To be at home in any awkward key means that one can concentrate one's efforts upon rhythm and style, for instance, and take in one's stride any sight-reading difficulties.

For those players, and that includes most of us who lack the tenacity to go through all the scales from memory, I would recommend the section in Part 1 of the *Méthode Complète* by André Lafosse (Leduc, Paris) where scales are set out in a very sensible way in somewhat extended form. Students would be well advised to work through these pages, and professionals to continue to do so regularly.

Chromatic scales on the trombone present a problem which in a way sums up the main technical difficulties of the instrument—making long slide movements as effectively and as accurately as very short ones. Here the comparisons are between the longest slide movements, 1–7, and adjacent positions.

My own suggested method of overcoming what so many players seem to find a great problem is to practise chromatic scales in groups of 6 notes (3 × 2), starting first on low E to A followed by another group from B♭ to E♭, insisting on accuracy even if this means practising continuously at a slow tempo. When this scale is mastered to, say, high B♭ and back again to low E a good degree of facility should have been achieved (*Note:* it is important for the slide to remain *stationary* for the duration of each note. A continuously gliding motion will result in continuously variable intonation, and is to be avoided.)

The next stage is to learn exactly the same progression but a semitone higher, starting on low F. Now the long slide movement 1–7 is in a different place in the scale. This should be practised in exactly the same way, slowly at first, minimizing the long slide-movement difficulties. This is followed by the same exercise on F♯, G, A♭, and A. The top augmented 4th may be omitted on the last two or three scales.

These scales are very difficult to play well and fast, but once learned, will remove all chromatic problems and improve the handling of the mechanics of the instrument. They can also be used effectively with B♭ and F instruments. Learning six different scales—they are different because of the varied requirements of co-ordination and short-v-long movements—can be a real boost to technical facility and the co-ordination of tongue and hand.

(Intonation tendencies which should be corrected in scale practice are movements 1–3–5–7 or 2–4–6, or combinations of these which tend to get flatter as the slide extends, and 7–5–3–1 or 6–4–2 which tend to cause sharpness when ascending.)

Alternative positions

It will not be long before the beginner realizes that the positions which he has learned in the most elementary stages of his playing, for middle E and above, are not the only ones which can be used. As one ascends into the upper register the possibility of duplicating notes in different positions increases greatly. This can be easily checked with the chart.

The tone quality of some of the lesser-used alternative positions may well vary from instrument to instrument, usually becoming less reliable as they ascend in the harmonic series. This is often a matter of use and familiarity, however, and although some players often seem to lack the courage to use extended positions, continued practice in their use will soon give more confidence.

There are, I believe, three main factors to consider when deciding which position to use for any given note—convenience, intonation, and tone quality.

Every player should have complete command of *all* the alternative positions. He should be capable of playing D F G A in 4th position for instance, with the necessary tuning adjustments, and similarly E♭ F G A in 6th. These are, of course, much more difficult and require more considerable

SHARPS   **FLATS**

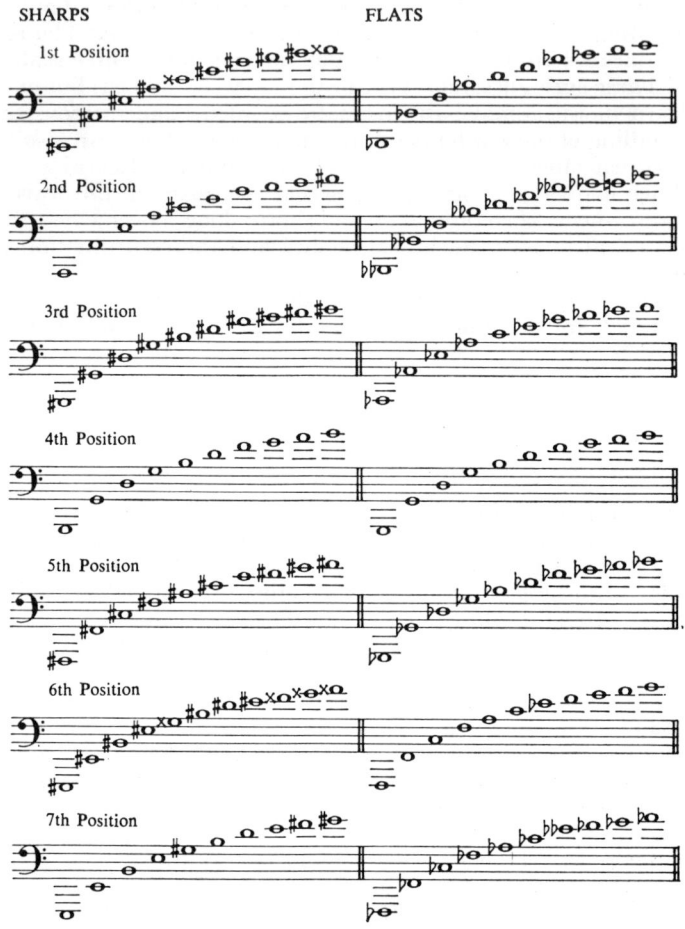

corrections which are, in any case, exaggerated in the furthest positions. This use of the comparatively less reliable upper harmonics of the long positions is absolutely essential in playing high glissandos reliably.

Of more general use is the range of 3rd, 4th, and 5th position notes, and every student should make it his business to be at least conversant with the notes from D 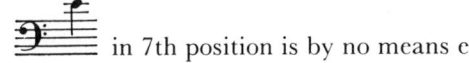 upwards

which can be obtained around the middle positions. To give a few examples at random, the Bb in 3rd and 5th, the E

in long 3rd and the high F in long 2nd or 4th

are really useful notes on occasions, more especially in legato playing.

The fact remains, however, that many young players fight shy of using positions that were not the original ones specified in their first tutor or study book. I usually recommend, in these cases, the exclusive use for a few days of, say, D and F in 4th positions and Bb and Db in 5th with the proper slide corrections for intonation—at first the intonation may well be faulty and the sound quality unequal to the usual positions. But perseverance will bring continued improvement, and will help not only in dexterity but also legato playing, and should increase the overall richness of tone in the more conventional positions.

I recommend practising the same note in different positions at all dynamics. Making a really good *ff* sound on upper E

in 7th position is by no means easy, and the required

embouchure and breath control can add surprisingly to the quality of sound on nearer positions. (*Recommended Study Material*: Lafosse part 1, preparatory exercises to glissando and preparatory exercises to legato (same notes, different positions).)

Pedal notes

The fundamental or 'pedal' notes, the lowest which can be played on any brass instrument, are used only rarely. They have a curious soft quality, unless blown very hard, and can, in the right circumstances, sound very beautiful. In *ff* they can sound terrifying!

A very relaxed embouchure is needed to produce these notes, with plenty of projection of the bottom jaw and lip. Many players *can* make the pedal notes work, but only by making some sort of embouchure change, and then there is no real control. I would emphasize that a properly working embouchure must give complete command of this register, so that it can be used just as any other part of the trombone's range. It should be possible to slur easily into and out of the 'pedal' register. If this cannot be done without altering the position of the mouthpiece on the embouchure, then there is a need to examine closely the embouchure structure and the advice of a good teacher must urgently be sought.

Of course, not every player can control the entire range down to pedal C (on the Bb and F trombone). Any player who is of a good standard should, however, be able to play down to F in the way I have described.

If this does not work, then I suggest the following exercises:
(1) Play a low Bb, with a carefully observed 'corners down' embouchure, and aim for the best possible tone-quality.
(2) When this is established, make a downward *lip* glissando, *very slowly*, until the lower octave is reached. The pedal note will eventually sound on what is basically the same embouchure (except for projected bottom jaw and lip) as the octave above. It should be then comparatively simple to slur this octave up and down, repeating the lip-glissando idea when the downward slur 'sticks'. The same process may be extended further down the entire range of fundamental notes. Bass trombonists (and tuba players) can benefit particularly from this simple study.

Many composers for the symphony orchestra have used trombone pedal notes, notably Berlioz, in the *Te Deum* and *Grande Messe des Morts*. Elgar, too, had a fondness for this rather unearthly sound.

Staccato

A precise, neat staccato is an absolute necessity on the trombone, as on all other instruments. If we consider the true meaning of staccato, the physical problem can be systematically solved. A staccato note should appear merely as a section of a long note, for staccato does not mean 'accent'. Therefore, the co-ordination of embouchure and tongue needs to be carefully organized. Very often, a young player will try to do something 'extra' with his tongue in order to make a staccato note start precisely when he wants it. If a note—at whatever dynamic—tends not to 'come out' to order, the fault *can* be traced to the position of the tongue.

The difficulty, however, is much more likely to be caused by the embouchure itself. In other words the lips may not begin to vibrate at the required moment in time. The remedy here is to practise a 'ha' production with an *fp* attack. If the embouchure is not properly arranged for any given note, there will be difficulties in starting the notes. Once the embouchure is properly lined up for any given note, it will respond to very much less effort, and eventually to hardly any. It remains then to make sure that the tongue makes a clean seal (see remarks on tonguing).

The usual problem encountered is that the tongue is sometimes used to stop the note with a 'tut', or more often, to 'pre-select' the next one. These procedures should be avoided for a really clean staccato. 'Tuh' or 'teh' are suggested syllables to correct these faults. The glottis should snap closed as soon as the note has begun; a tiny diminuendo on all but the very shortest of notes is a pleasing musical effect, and happens quite naturally when the glottis closes a fraction slower than instantaneously.

To sum up, staccato needs;

(1) a really precise production
(2) enough breath support to give the note sufficient quality to ring
(3) an almost immediate closure of the glottis.

Practising with a 'ha' articulation, as suggested above, also helps the glottis close properly to complete the note.

Legato

The trombone has infinite possibilities for legato playing, which can be at least as effective as those of the valved brass instruments or indeed the woodwind. The human voice is probably the only musical instrument that is better equipped. This does not mean, however, that legato-playing is easy on the trombone. On the contrary, it is very difficult, and its mastery needs a great deal of thought and practice to make it always *sound* very easy!

The basis of good legato playing on the trombone is that the flow of air, and therefore, the sound, should be completely continuous, and that the notes must be so long as almost to merge with one another. Any sounds between legato notes must be completely eliminated (unless a 'portamento' effect is desired). Therefore a prerequisite for a perfect legato is a fast, smooth, and precise slide movement. Let us consider the various possible ways of producing a good legato on the trombone:

(1) *Natural slurs in the same or near-by positions.* These are, of course, produced similarly on all brass instruments. By going through the appropriate embouchure and diaphragm mechanisms, as already described, it is possible to learn to *slur*—i.e. change notes of the harmonic series smoothly without altering the tube length. Some slurs are obviously more difficult than others, but every combination should be worked on, and, if possible, perfected. Incidentally, slurring with clean legato movements in the same position is probably the most beneficial single type of practice that a trombonist can undertake. It puts in a nutshell as it were the control of the complex muscular structures of the orbicularis oris; in long slurs, the muscles have to snap into the next note-shape, with, in theory at any rate, no time at all in which to do so. The same movements also occur in ordinary detached playing, of course, but there is usually more time to make them. Although the exercises on p. 53 are not intended as suggestions to composers, they are examples of the kind of slurring that is necessary and indeed essential, for the student to practise.

Similar exercises, with movements to near-by positions, are also included in this category.

(2) *Moving the slide in the opposite direction to that of the notes.* This is an equally valid method of making a good legato between neighbouring notes. This again subdivides into two types:

(a) inwards with the slide, downwards with the notes. This is one of the most gratifying aspects of trombone playing, for it is a very reliable way of producing an excellent legato. Intonation of the upper note may be a problem if it is in a not often used position. In very loud playing it is also very difficult and not so effective.

(b) outwards with the slide and upwards with the notes. This is much more difficult. It is generally inadvisable below middle B♭, and very often only effective above that note. In the upper register, however, the most beautiful horn-like slurs are possible this way. Louder dynamics make this valve-type slur less smooth than Legato-tonguing.

(3) *Legato-tonguing.* By observing the cardinal rule that in a true legato the airstream is never broken, it is possible, and in fast playing desirable, to have a dependable method of placing legato notes by assisting them with the tongue. This articulation, or rather semi-articulation, is made by stroking the tip of the tongue at varying angles on the part of the roof of the mouth about ½ in. behind the gum line.

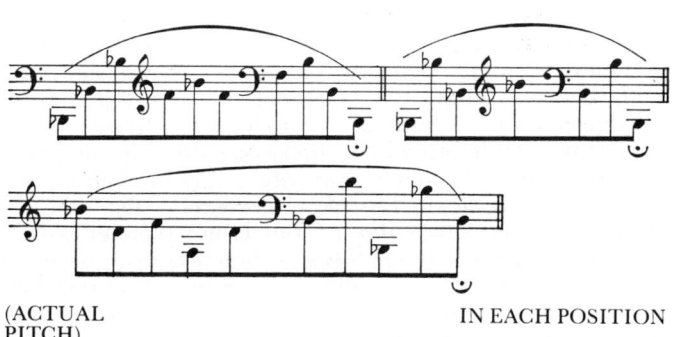

(ACTUAL
PITCH)   IN EACH POSITION

Varying syllables are suggested: 'thee, thoo, thaw' both as in 'this' and as in 'thing', and 'lee, loo, law' or 'nee, noo, naw', or 'rrroo, rrree, rrraw' like the beginning of a rolled 'rrr'. Each of these, or possible even more, will be found of use for most players. Some players prefer a mixture of the above suggestions. Using these with others provides different effects in legato comparable to the many nuances that a good string-player can make with differing kinds of bow-action.

4) *Tongue-less Legato*. Under certain conditions—at low dynamics, for instance—it is possible and often effective to play a passage as if one were legato-tonguing, but without any tongue action at all. The slide must, of course, be nimble and the breath (diaphragm and glottis) well controlled. If these conditions are all fulfilled this can sound very fine; it is only available to the advanced player, when its use is really just a matter of personal choice or taste.

To sum up, there are four basic ways of making a really controlled musical legato on the trombone which are easily accessible to the student. It has been my experience that 'natural' slurs are, especially when properly practised and developed, the cleanest and most satisfying. All other methods of making legato must approximate to the best natural slur, which remains a yardstick for comparison. The student must match absolutely the various ways of making his legato, so that there is no audible difference between them.

So often, melodic trombone playing sounds like a valiant performer on a difficult instrument 'getting by'. It is axiomatic that unless a special effect is being consciously sought, any sounds between legato notes are not only unnecessary but downright unmusical, and to be avoided absolutely.

One of the odd habits which otherwise extremely competent players may have is that of the 'egg' or 'pear-shaped' note when playing *legato* or *sostenuto*. It seems to me that this distortion usually comes about through lack of confidence in legato ability, somehow confused with a desire to play with great expression. Notes usually begin with the embouchure slightly too closed, and the note gradually strengthens as it 'centres' and becomes a little fuller and louder as it continues.

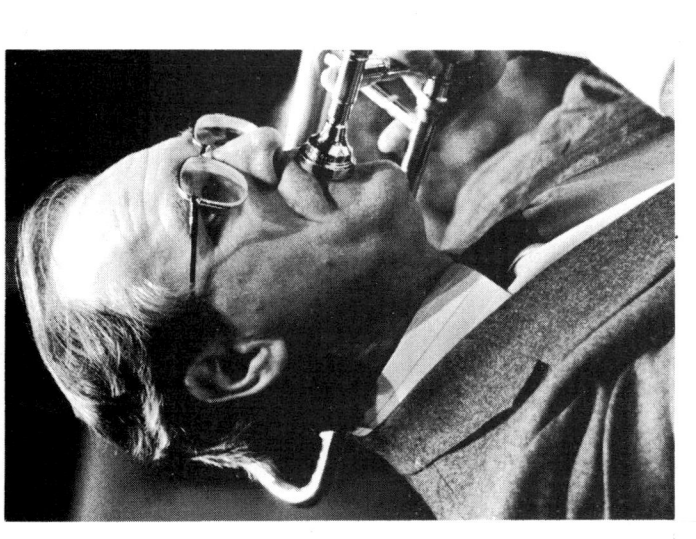

2 Main features of the mouthpiece

Shank

Backbore

Throat

Rim

Cup

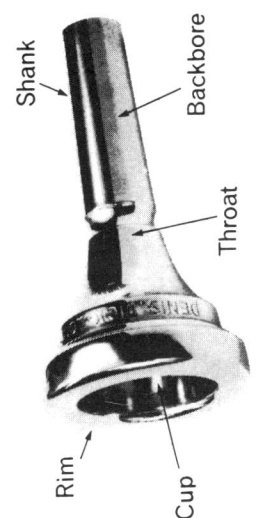

1 Correct embouchure, demonstrated by the author (see page 16)

3 1st position

4 4th position with wrist straight,
   fingers pivoting

These illustrations show possible variations of the right hand position. There are two basic systems. One pivots at the wrist, one at the fingers. Both 1st and 7th positions are reached in exactly the same way with either system.

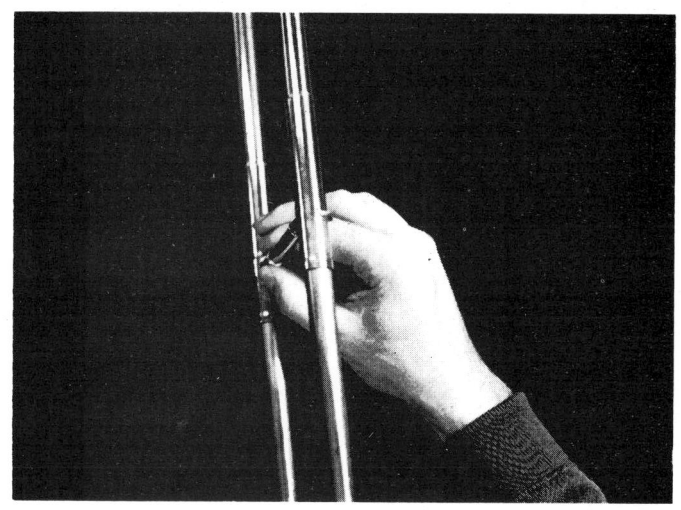

6 6th position with wrist straight, fingers pivoting

5 4th position with wrist at an angle, relative finger position unchanged

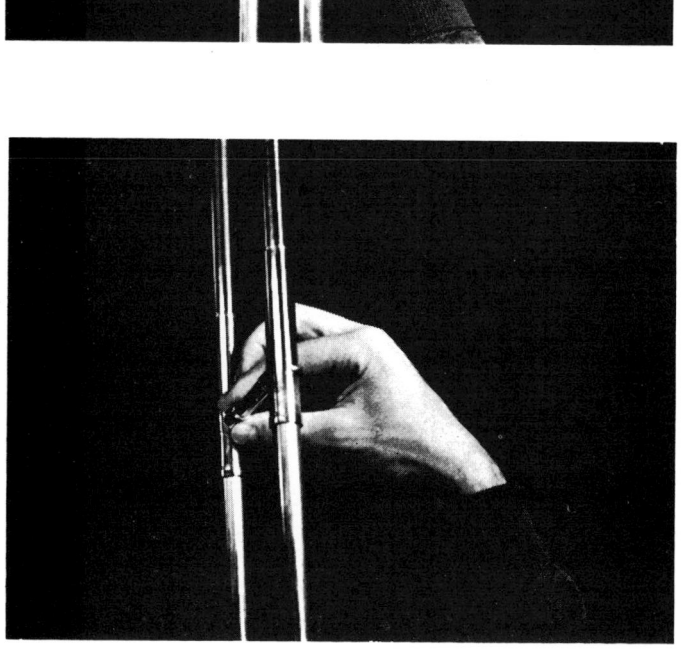

7 6th position with wrist at an angle, relative position of fingers unchanged

8 7th position: the need to reach the full length of the slide brings the hand into the same position for either system

Basically this is an uncorrected embouchure fault, which sometimes persists with players who are otherwise well developed. It goes without saying that this style—or distortion of style—makes real phrasing an impossibility and is completely at variance with modern ideas of orchestral playing.

Perhaps the trombone is not quite as prone to this fault as are other brass instruments on which legato playing is easier. In his efforts to make a good legato with fast slide-movements and ultra-smooth lip slurs, the properly-taught trombonist is likely to be very conscious of 'pear-shaped' notes, and will probably not encounter the problem.

For some obscure reason loud legato playing tends to be neglected in practice—probably because of its difficulty. Many composers have written this as a tutti melodic line, which was only doubled on trombone, and some examples come to mind which need to be given the same kind of treatment as in soft playing, but with more air support.

The following passages need preparing at no more than *mf*, increasing dynamics slowly to the required *f* and *ff*:

Britten, *Peter Grimes*; 'Storm' from the 'Sea Interludes', including figs. 3-4, 5-6, 13-end (3rd part):

Britten, *Spring Symphony*:

This unison passage has certain notes left out of each part, which greatly facilitates its execution.

The 'outwards and upwards' legato-type, discussed above (type 2 (b)), is generally a viable method of tongue-less legato only in the upper register of the trombone. Here, however, really smooth progressions are possible. They are much beloved of studio, jazz, and dance-music players, who make really beautiful contrasts between valve-like slurs in contrary motion and 'portamento' in similar motion. To the symphonic player, whose excursions into these realms are necessarily rare, they are a matter of some envy, and much private practice! However, he needs all the possible resources of legato technique to give cantabile performances of Ravel's *Bolero* or even of the 4th movement of Schumann's 3rd Symphony for instance.

(The studio player has distinct advantages in using smaller equipment (see p.1). He needs a far narrower dynamic range and has much greater freedom of expression than the symphonic trombonist in the concert hall.)

An interesting addition to the possibilities of legato on the trombone, and available to players with good high register control, is an extension of the possibilities of free slurring. Here are some examples:

Few composers have exploited this better then Benjamin Britten, who in *A Midsummer Night's Dream* and, more obviously in the 'Sanctus' of the *War Requiem*, uses it with brilliant effect.

It may be worth mentioning that when playing legato very softly there is likely to be some disturbance of the air column when making long slide movements. Although very smooth, modern slides are almost airtight. The slide, of course, will only act as a pump if the end of the tube is closed; there is, however, a tendency for long inward slide movements to compress the air a little, possibly causing a slight involuntary crescendo. More dangerously, long outward movements can give the feeling that there is not enough flow of air to keep the note going. Mutes, particularly those with a cork-ring, intensify these tendencies. In practice, most players very soon develop a natural way of counter-balancing them and should take them very much in their stride. The kind of technique that is, in any case, necessary for a really good legato should be able to cope with them without too much trouble.

The following two examples of well-known difficult solos for trombone show my suggested positions: a smooth overall effect should be achieved by using natural slurs whenever possible. I have indicated where I would use a perfectly matched legato tongue ('L').

The trombone phrasing is Mozart's in the last three bars, mine elsewhere.

In the next example, the composer avoids phrasing indications, simply suggesting 'sostenuto'. Any awkwardness can be removed from this solo by playing it in a 'semi-legato' style, and by using the positions suggested.

Trills

Although not the novelty that they once were, trills are still found very difficult by many young players. They are made simply by slurring rapidly with the lip between two notes on adjacent harmonic series. The minute movements of the lower lip which can be so useful in making clean, smooth lip-slurs, have to be made precisely and accurately, and not exaggerated. Students often try to make too much movement with the supporting muscles. This should be discouraged, and the centre of the embouchure should make all the movement necessary. There is no real short cut; trills must be practised, slowly at first, then faster, until they eventually acquire the kind of even quality to be found in trills made by woodwind and valved brass instruments. Quite apart from the need to be able to play trills in solos and in the limited number of orchestral pieces that need them, they are excellent practice in themselves, and practised *loudly* can improve the strength of the embouchure.

For completeness, I include a table of possible trills on the trombone:

With a regular rhythmic pulse, trills should be practised in the following way:

Vibrato

The ability to make a beautiful controlled vibrato is a very necessary part of the trombonist's technique. Vibrato, the undulation of the sound a fraction of a semitone above and/or below the written pitch, can be obtained on the trombone in several ways, some of which are to be recommended, others not:

(1) *Slide vibrato* is customarily used by many fine jazz trombone players. The hand and wrist should be supple, neither stiff nor really loose. For vibrato the hand moves in a fast but controllable way; the distance travelled by the slide will probably vary between players (and different current styles) from about ¾ to 1½ in. The actual speed of vibrato will vary for the same reasons. Slide vibrato has certain inherent snags. In first position vibrato is virtually impossible—Tommy Dorsey is said never to have used 1st position in any of his solos for this reason—and in 6th or 7th positions would also be somewhat awkward. The vibrato produced in this way by experts is a really beautiful sound, which is difficult to improve upon in any of the other methods.

(2) *Diaphragm vibrato* is possibly the best way to imitate vocal technique and, if carefully studied, can impart a singing quality to solo passages.

(3) *Lip vibrato* which may be approached rather like the beginning of a lip trill (q.v.) and which can be controlled very easily, approximating to, though never quite matching, slide vibrato.

(4) *Throat vibrato* is an outmoded 'nanny-goat' effect made by interrupting the flow of air at the glottis. This was very popular and much used thirty or more years ago. It is still very occasionally heard, but is not to be encouraged.

(5) *Head vibrato*—A vertical shaking of the head which produces the same effect as a lip vibrato in a much more cumbersome way. Generally not to be encouraged.

To sum up. Trombonists whose work is likely to be solely in dance-type music would do well to perfect a good slide-vibrato. Band players should use a well-controlled, tasteful, slower diaphragm-vibrato for solo playing. Symphonic players should be able to provide a fast, French-type lip vibrato, a slower vocal-type diaphragm vibrato, and, if possible, have a really beautiful slide vibrato also at their disposal.

Other forms of vibrato are not really comparable to the above, and their use should be discouraged.

Flutter tongue

This effect on the trombone, not particularly difficult to learn, is made by rolling an 'r' with the tongue. It has been used since the nineteenth century, and today it is beloved of film composers to make an *ff* sound devastatingly loud. Used with mute, it becomes more subtle. Richard Strauss, in *Don Quixote*, made his muted flutter-tonguing brass into a very amusing flock of sheep.

It was for a time the trade mark of the twelve-note composers of the earlier period who liked to score odd notes *ppp* flutter-tongue (con sordino). Although it is comparatively original, it should be pointed out that in the upper register it becomes very difficult to control when played very softly.

When flutter-tonguing is used continuously, each note should not be articulated with a separate definition, with a short rest before the note, unless specifically written.

Flutter-tongue has to be continued or the effect is spoiled:

It would perhaps be more logical if there were a legato-line over the whole passage:

The glissando

With its infinitely variable tube-length it is not surprising that the trombone is probably the chief source of the glissando in the orchestra, equalled perhaps only by stringed instruments. The effect has been somewhat over-used, especially in popular arrangements of the 1920s and 1930s. Most serious composers and good orchestrators tend to use the glissando very sparingly indeed, and the effect, which is really more startling and bizarre than musical, is more striking when not overworked.

There are no real problems in making a glissando, the slide simply travels more slowly, and breaks the legato 'rule'—there *has* to be continuity of sound between the notes. Care should be taken that the slow slide-movements are not jerked in any way. Glissandos starting from first or near-by positions are easy, but there are some difficulties in beginning with unaccustomed notes in extended positions. It is in any case worth practising alternate positions, but being able to play in tune a solid E♭ in 6th of F♯ in 5th will make any glissando possible. The Lafosse *Méthode Complète* offers some excellent studies in preparation for glissando, which are designed to strengthen the long-position upper register. I strongly recommend these exercises and the glissando exercises themselves.

Some composers seem to have very strange ideas as to what glissandos are possible. The following table of glissandos can easily be worked out, but it may save time to include it. I also include the increased number of glissandos which are made possible by use of the 'F' valve.

Example:

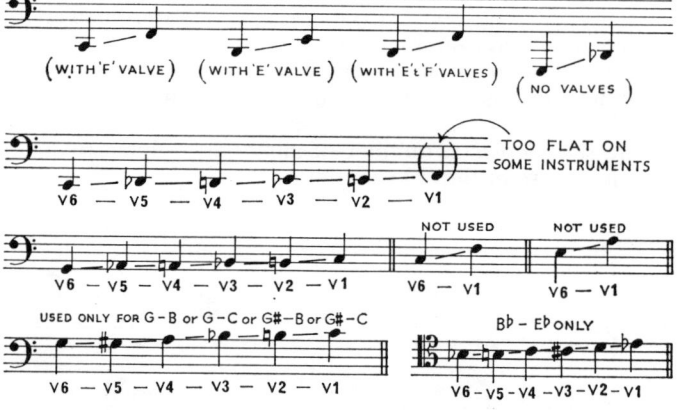

Stravinsky in *Firebird*, Walton in the *Scapino* Overture, and Ravel at the end of *Bolero*, all have fine examples of how to use the glissando to maximum effect. There are, unfortunately, just as many examples in less brilliant compositions where the impossible is expected. As ever, necessity is the mother of invention, and most players work out their own compromises for glissandos which should never have been written.

Here are two examples of particularly difficult glissandos:

(1) Debussy—*Iberia* ('Jour de Fêtes'—last 3 bars, 3 trombone parts)—Durand

Positions used:

    1st D (7th) gliss, F♯ (3rd), lip gliss B (4th)
                                         gliss D (1st)
    2nd B (7th) gliss, D♯ (3rd), lip gliss G♯ (5th)
                                         gliss B (2nd)
    3rd G (4th) lip gliss, D (7th) gliss G (2nd)

(2) Elgar—*Cockaigne Overture*

    Fig. 30—31, 1st and 2nd trombones 'glissez fantastico'

In the Debussy, the effect is of a breathtaking full octave glissando; Elgar merely wanted to suggest an early jazz-band by hinting at it vaguely in an accompaniment.

The harsh loud glissando is an outworn cliché which should be used very rarely indeed. Very few composers however seem to have considered the rather wistful *pp* glissando, which is rather beautiful and by no means overworked.

F bass trombone glissando

The F bass trombone was the instrument that Béla Bartók had in mind in the *Concerto for Orchestra* and *The Miraculous Mandarin*. Both these pieces use glissando very effectively

indeed.   The *Concerto for Orchestra* has B-F,

easily playable on the F bass trombone but not so easily on the B♭ and F. The solutions are either to use a B♭-F-E trombone, and let the E valve lever come up at the beginning or end of the glissando, or to 'lip' down the low C, that the B♭ and F can make in 7th position, to a B. This is done quite easily, by projecting the lower lip and by careful aural adjustment. The sound, however, is likely to be inferior, and the B♭ two-valve bass trombone is the only real solution in modern terms. The other possibility, of course, is to use the F bass trombone as originally intended.

Clefs

To the amateur, the fact that trombone music may be found in bass, tenor, alto, or treble clefs is often confusing enough to make some music which he could otherwise cope with quite unavailable to him. Let us first consider the concert-pitch or non-transposing clefs. The two C clefs, tenor and alto, stand in different parts of their respective staves, but in each case middle C goes through the middle of the clef sign.

ALTO   TENOR

These clefs are used in symphony orchestras and represent the actual pitch of the played note. Very occasionally the treble clef is also used, also denoting the actual sounds made.

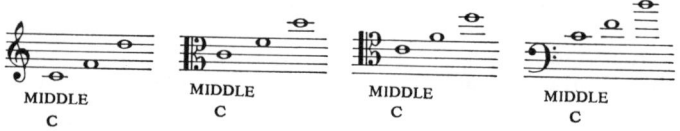

MIDDLE MIDDLE MIDDLE MIDDLE
C   C   C   C

Just to complicate matters even more there exists also a transposing treble clef, in which the notes are written a 9th higher than they sound. The British brass band almost always scores in this way, and a number of solos and studies are written in this '9th notation'.

It does not need much research to reveal that notes written in tranposing treble clef have exactly the same sound and appearance as those in tenor clef. The only difference is of key and of the name of the note so that C in treble clef is B♭ in Tenor, not B♮, and similarly F in treble clef is E♭ in tenor. Brass band players who have sometimes to read in either clef will be familiar with this procedure—they just subtract two flats from the tenor clef or add two to the treble clef. This short cut is really cheating—often they even call tenor-clef notes by treble-clef names.

Occasionally one may find parts for a tranposed bass clef

'Trombone in B♭' in Continental band parts. This applies also to the Richard Strauss parts for tenor tuba. They have to be tranposed down one whole tone to be made to sound at concert pitch. (See the chapter on the euphonium.)

One extraordinary fact about scoring for the brass band has always puzzled me. The only two instruments written in the bass clef are the bass (originally G) trombone and the percussion. The reasons for this are, one imagines, to enable bandsmen to interchange instruments with the minimum of difficulty. This is understandable, for any given note in treble clef meant the same fingering and had the same pitch relationship on each instrument. For some reason however this never reached the G trombone, and the player of this instrument had to work out his own way of reading, which corresponds to none of the tricks of clef/transposition.

Dance-music, stage-band music, and so on, is always written in concert pitch bass clef. This has always seemed to me somewhat unreasonable when the range of the upper parts will scarcely ever descend into the bass clef, and nearly always appear as leger lines. Surely, concert-pitch treble clef would save the copyist a great deal of time, and be easier to read into the bargain! One does not even have to consider such exotica as alto or tenor clefs. Everyone knows what a treble clef is, and it should not take long for the trombonist to reorientate himself into concert-pitch treble.

There is an additional factor too, which is purely psychological, although none the less important. High notes that look high are much harder than high notes that do not. I have found no real problem in high notes in alto or concert-pitch treble, but the 'telegraph poles' of high parts written in bass clef always seem frightening!

Transposition

The trombonist will very rarely encounter the problems of transposition that orchestral horn and trumpet players have to cope with all the time. A working knowledge of the four clefs will cover all his reading problems, but a good musician should not find it difficult to read parts for horn in E♭ (which is bass clef one octave higher) or F, which may be regarded as alto clef + 3rd, tenor + 5th, or bass + 9th.

I strongly recommend every player to learn the clefs which he does not use in his normal playing. The brass band player should learn bass clef, the jazz or stage-band performer should learn tenor and alto. In this way they may at least give themselves the chance of a broader outlook, and a much wider range of solos and, even more important, study material.

Chords and other unusual sounds

It has been known at least since the time of Weber that it is possible to make a brass instrument give more than one note at a time. This is done by humming or singing into the instrument while simultaneously playing. The sung note must be in tune with one of the harmonic partials present on the played note. The trombone seems to be a good instrument for making this 'magic' and I have known one or two trombonists who have been able to perform chords very successfully. It certainly comes as a surprise to an audience!

Once again, careful study and practice aimed at perfecting the intonation and balance of the two notes is needed before the 'chords' appear properly—when they do, more notes than the one played and the one sung can be heard—sometimes even two or three more. A tape recorder and much patience are suggested as practice-aids.

Although most trombonists are much too busy playing real notes to have time to spend on this somewhat freakish effect, one can but admire the patience of those few players who can make it into an artistic part of their playing, and who can then use it in solos. So far no composer has used this 'trick' in orchestral music.

All kinds of weird extra-musical effects can be made on the trombone, by singing, whistling, shouting, or gurgling into the instrument, not to mention striking the bell with the mouthpiece or closing both ends of the slide section (having taken off the bell) and making an explosion by pulling the outer slide off sharply. (This actually happens in a recent piece, *Bolos*, for four trombones, by the Swedish composers Bark and Rabe.)

Who knows what trombonists of the future will be expected to do?

The trombone in 'avant-garde' music

The late 1960s have seen several compositions featuring the trombone as soloist which use all the above effects and possibly more. The 'Sequenza V' of 'Luciano Berio (1966) is probably the most well known of these pieces and has inspired subsequent compositions of similar genre by such composers as Vinko Globakar (a trombonist himself) Karlheinz Stockhausen, Carlos Roqué Alsina, J.Krastavitsa, and J.Druckman. Whilst exploring unimagined regions of sound—the rubber plunger mute, the spoken and sung voice in the instrument, as well as played sounds, this music requires as much in the way of stage presence (in the 'Sequenza V') and histrionic imagination and inventiveness as it does technique. It seems unlikely to me that this kind of music will ever reach or be enjoyed by a very wide public, but it has certainly aroused a great deal of interest among trombonists, particularly of the younger generation.

The comparisons between the trombone and the human voice, of which it must be regarded as an extension, are quite fascinating. I would suggest that this kind of playing should only be attempted when every other aspect of the trombone has been completely mastered. There are some excellent preparatory exercises for 'multiphonics' by Donald Appert.

SUPPLEMENTARY EQUIPMENT

The F valve

The idea of an additional length of tubing that could be added or subtracted from the trombone at will, probably has its ancestry in the use of crooks to pitch the various brass instruments in different keys. The invention of the rotary valve and its adoption in nineteenth-century central Europe made the Bb and F trombone a natural development. The F tubing is added to the main tube of the instrument by actuating the rotary valve by means of the thumb of the left hand. Early examples of this idea had the F tube leading directly from the mouthpiece end of the instrument, with the valve actuated by the left forefinger. This was regarded as acoustically the best position for it. However, it became more practical to install the valve with its 2½ feet of tubing in the bell-section of the instrument.

The German and Bohemian instruments of the time had longish slides and comparatively short bell-sections, and the convention became, and still is, to place the F valve in the lower part of the tuning slide, and to have a long chain with a leather thong at the end which could be adjusted and operated with the left thumb. The advantage of this is that the whole tuning slide, plus valve and tubing, could be replaced with a plain tuning slide.

Fashions change, however, and modern instrument makers place the F valve immediately behind the player's left hand, the valve being activated directly by the thumb with a simple lever and either string or mechanical linkage. The amount of tubing added is equal to extending the slide to the sixth position. This not only makes it theoretically unnecessary to use 6th and 7th positions, but brings into play a whole range of new possibilities, and can be used to bridge the gap between the fundamental (pedal) note and the first harmonic when both lengths of tubing (F valve and main slide) are used together. The F valve tubing also has an adjustable tuning slide.

There are, however, several problems that arise from these undoubtedly beneficial possibilities.

(1) The sound on the F valve notes is rarely as good as those made on the slide alone.

(2) A low F register which is equal in quality, strength, flexibility, and control to the B♭ notes has to be achieved by hard work, though it can be done.

(3) Most important of all, the trombone slide has only six positions when the F valve is being used.

Let us deal with the last point first. The six positions relate to the seven positions of the B♭ instrument as follows (the seven positions are numbered above the line, the six positions with the F valve below the line).

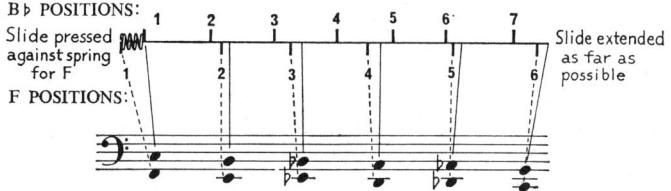

It will be seen from this diagram that harmonics in the same position as the 1st harmonic notes tend to be sharp. They need to be flattened as shown. Many bass trombonists forgo the 1st position F in order to facilitate the low C, especially if they have a short right arm.

The reason for there being only six positions is not hard to see. When the instrument is pitched in F instead of B♭, a greater length of tubing is needed to add the notes which the slide gives. Thus only six semitones can be added by the B♭ slide. Even then the sixth position is so far extended as to be located on the last inch or so of the slide. There is no possibility of playing the B♮ one semitone above the fundamental—the slide is just one position too short.

Many manufacturers offer an alternative 'E' position for the F valve tuning slide, which has some 9 or 10 in. of parallel tubing, giving a 'pull' of nearly 18 in. in extra tube length. French-made bass trombones have in fact always been built in B♭ and E thus giving a completely chromatic low register and a more easily assimilated comparison between the new 6 positions and the old 7.

Some instrument-makers have carried this a stage further by introducing B♭, F and E trombones, with two valves and an additional length of tube which loops from the F valve tubing activated by the extra valve. Since the second valve cannot be used independently of the first, the valve levers have to be so arranged that when the E valve is depressed, both valves are activated. It also has to allow easy movement from one valve to two or vice-versa. One manufacturer, Frank Holton & Co., realizing that the bass trombonist needs the low B♮ very infrequently, has made an optional F valve tuning slide, which itself contains another valve, to add the extra semitone. This is discussed in the chapter on the bass trombone—so far no tenor trombones have been made in this way.

It has usually been the custom to make the F tubing of a larger bore than that of the main slide of the trombone because this was thought to give greater fullness to the lower F register notes. The newer idea of keeping the bore size the same seems to have disproved this theory, and the F valve notes now actually respond more evenly, and are more compatible with the B♭ register. It would seem that this has to do with the ratio of bore-size *after* the F valve, when there needs to be a comparatively sudden increase in bore size.

It has been claimed by at least one authority that the invention of the F valve gives the trombone the same possibilities as the double horn, and is just as revolutionary for the technique of the instrument. With this I wholeheartedly disagree. I concede that the F side of the instrument is by no means a makeshift; in fact, the sound from it can be made to match the B♭ side very well. However, in the middle and upper register, the use of the F valve tends to give a sound more like that of a small bore euphonium or baritone than that of a trombone. There are indeed one or two occasions when it may prove unexpectedly useful. The following examples are more in the nature of trick effects, but they show how at *ff* level the baritone quality can even be an advantage.

Verdi *Requiem*—'Dies Irae':

Arthur Bliss—*Beatitudes*:

    It can, therefore, be said that the F valve is most useful below middle (bass clef) F, and its use is generally to be avoided above this.

Mutes

In the symphony orchestra, mutes are of two kinds, metal and fibre. Both of these come under the generic name of 'straight' mute. In dance and commercial music there are also many other variations of mutes: cup mute, mega-mute, harmon-mute, solo-tone mute, bucket-mute, bowler hat plunger, hush-mute, and so on. In general these types fall into three categories:

    (1) those with three corks that permit air to flow between the mute and the bell;

    (2) those with a cork ring that seal off the air at this point and make it flow through the mute itself;

    (3) the bucket-shaped extension which clips on the bell and muffles the sound in this way, or the bowler hat and the plunger which are held against the bell.

    The cup-mute consists of the fibre or metal 'straight' mute with a cup-shape like a deep saucer fixed to the end of it. It should be adjusted so that it is about ¼ in. from the bell. Of the cork-ring mutes the harmon-mute is most often used. It has a movable tube, which may be removed completely, giving a smooth round sound, or extended, giving a piercing nasal quality. It may, of course, also be left in, when a more compact nasal sound results. The other forms of 'hush', 'mega', and 'solotone' are all special names given to mutes which also seal off the air with a cork ring and are thus able to influence the tone colour with variously shaped tubes and cones. They all have the same *kind* of pleasant clear quality, but they are all slightly different.

In the symphony orchestra, it is usual to have at least two straight mutes, of contrasting sound qualities. Metal mutes are usually very clear and harsh in dynamics of *mf* upwards. They are most useful in the kind of cutting *ff* writing found in works of many modern composers—e.g. Stravinsky (*Firebird, Rite of Spring*). They also have excellent qualities of flexibility at low dynamic levels. The fibre mutes are better for more discreet effects, and make a tighter sound in *mf* and less, when 'mute' *does* mean a softer, not just a changed sound quality.

It is essential to acquire mutes that really suit the instrument for which they are intended. Corks should be carefully adjusted so that the full range of the instrument can be played with an even muted quality. This applies particularly to Bb and F tenor and bass trombones, where the F valve notes are prone to give trouble with a mute.

Mute corks usually need to be sandpapered down a little, to give a clear and even sound, particularly on these low F valve notes. In doing this, the angle of the bell-flare should be followed closely, to give maximum grip. If the mute is too small for a particular trombone, there is likely to be a tendency towards sharpness of pitch. This becomes more evident when the corks are reduced to give the best sound-quality.

Right-handed players usually prefer to insert the mute with the right hand, holding the trombone, with slide closed, in the left. Left-handed or ambidextrous players usually insert and remove the mute with the left hand. This seems a more logical idea, as the left hand is often needed to hold the mute for a quick removal, or to operate the tube-end of a 'wa-wa' Harmon mute. A slight twist is enough to make the mute grip in the bell.

It is very desirable to put in the mute silently, especially when recording. I always try to slide it in with one of the corks touching the side of the bell, in order to avoid knocking the metal ferrule, if there is one, against the bell.

Trombone players are generally not as dexterous as trumpet players in quick mute changes, and composers' intentions are often disregarded if there is not very much time to mute. Orchestral players need to take a leaf from the book of their jazz colleagues, who are able to make miraculously quick changes. Composers should try to allow at least three seconds to put in the mute with perhaps a little less time to take it out, remembering that the more cumbersome kinds of mute are not as easy to control as the 'straight' mute.*

Practice mutes

In a completely different category are mutes made specifically for practice purposes. Most manufacturers offer mutes which reduce sound volume to almost nothing. Unfortunately they also distort intonation, especially when used with large bore instruments, and, of course, are worse than useless for practice purposes. With this problem in mind I have produced an extremely simple practice mute which retains normal intonation. This mute has the added advantage that, being made of metal, it gives a metallic 'buzz' when played loudly. For obvious reasons, most players do not normally practise at maximum volume. When occasionally they are called upon the play *fff*, all kinds of distortions of pitch, sound quality, and rhythm occur. If ten minutes or so per day are set aside for *fff* practice, using the pratice mute especially in the low register, and always maintaining careful control of the sound by listening to the 'buzz' of the mute, considerable improvement in other areas of playing will be achieved. The glottis is better controlled and the overall tone quality improves dramatically.

*Having tried for many years to find a metal mute that worked well in all registers, especially with the F valve in use, I have now designed and produced mutes for tenor and bass trombones that will play all the low notes and which do not sharpen the pitch. These mutes are now obtainable from Boosey & Hawkes or their dealers.

6

THE TROMBONE IN THE
SYMPHONY ORCHESTRA

Historical

The trombone has existed in more or less its present shape from the latter half of the sixteenth century, since when it has always maintained a place in the musical life of the cultural centres of Europe, and has been in use continuously in all kinds of music.

There are still in existence instruments made in the sixteenth century, and these can be played in the same way as modern trombones, although the slide mechanism is clumsy by modern standards. The quality of sound they can be made to produce is very pleasant although without much dynamic range. The design did not include the present-day bell-flare, and are similar to a modern trombone with perhaps three of four inches cut off the bell.

The first notable composer to use the trombone in concerted music was almost certainly Giovanni Gabrieli (1557–1612). At St. Mark's in Venice he had no less than six trombone players at his disposal. He used them to splendid effect in his *Symphoniae Sacrae*—music of a purely instrumental nature with two or more groups of instruments answering each other antiphonally as well as playing together. Many of these early examples of trombone writing are available in modern editions.

Since then virtually every composer has written for the trombone. Each of these composers had, it is natural to suppose, a somewhat different sound in mind when he scored for the trombones, and each composer poses a different problem for the modern symphonic trombonist.

Symphony orchestras today play a wider range of music than ever before, both historically and geographically. As trombonists, we are expected to make a clear yet warm sound (not loud) for Mozart and Beethoven, and warmer one for

Brahms and Bruckner, with a certain degree of brilliance in the first trombone part, warm with more character for Mahler and Strauss, a brilliant, but not overpowering sound for Elgar and Holst, and spiky, edgy playing for early Stravinsky and Ravel, with plenty of 'panache'. We must, therefore, have the will and ability completely to change our style and approach two or three times in an evening's performance. The most surprising aspect of this to the inexperienced player is that identical indications on the music very often mean completely different things. Weber, very often wrote *ff*, and the symphonic player, seeing this in *Der Freischütz* or *Oberon* has to realize that they were written for an opera pit orchestra with softer sounding alto, tenor and F bass trombones. If he is in a concert hall he must mentally 'mark down' his *f* and *ff* indications for these reasons.

Berlioz, who even now is regarded as perhaps the most brilliant and original orchestrator ever, in the first part of the nineteenth century used his trombones in the most varied and original ways:—with terrifying power (as in the *Symphonie Fantastique*), with great expression (*L'Enfance du Christ*), and with the awe-inspiring majesty of eight trombones playing unison pedal notes, in the *Grande Messe des Morts*. He, like most composers, was very much influenced by contemporary players and Antoine Dieppo, who was professor at the Paris Conservatoire from 1836–1871, was a major source of his ideas of what a trombone could do. Berlioz entrusted to him the fine funeral-oration solo in the *Grande Symphonie Funèbre et Triomphale*. Perhaps it is indicative of Berlioz's timelessness as an orchestrator, that in the modern symphony orchestra, with modern equipment, one can play the dynamics of his trombone parts *exactly* as written.

Wagner was also a great innovator, using trombones for many telling dramatic effects, particularly in *The Ring*. In the concert hall one has to remember that this music was written to be played in a covered orchestra pit; the louder dynamics therefore need great caution. Even more depth and breadth of sound are required than in Brahms or Bruckner and with hardly any 'edge'. The bass trumpet often supplies this 'edge', giving the brilliance which otherwise would be provided by the first trombone.

Dvorak gave the trombone really beautiful *pp* effects with a few interjections of chords and phrases. His music needs a warm yet resonant quality.

Mahler was important in that he brought forward the trombone from the back of the orchestra into an occasional solo position, as well as writing exquisitely for a section of three or four players. The first movement of his Third Symphony has recurring solo passages which project many varied aspects of the trombone. The character of the trombone fits in very well with the spirit of the music and the music similarly suits the character of the trombone. Mahler left nothing to chance and wrote precisely what he wanted. He was a tyrannical conductor who knew exactly what all the instruments of the orchestra could do and insisted on perfection. The trombone writing is not only extremely well done but also very rewarding to play. It is essential to understand, or have translated, his many interpretative directions.

Sibelius often gave the trombone dynamics which are generally a little too light. His own orchestra, which played his music when first written, was usually under-manned in the strings. In the last movement of his Second Symphony, the passage for two trombones (8 bars before R) is marked *mp* and is generally played at least *f*. There are similar instances to be found in most of his works. Sibelius used a solo trombone to declaim the main theme on each of its appearances in the one-movement Seventh Symphony. Here one needs an enormous, massive sound with really good breath control.

Schoenberg has written more difficult parts for trombone than had ever been thought feasible. I suspect that much of this was written in ignorance and hope! it is, of course, possible that the composer had the co-operation of a contemporary virtuoso. Today the technique required offers hardly any problem to a good player.

Berg on the other hand particularly in the *Three Orchestral Pieces* and the operas *Wozzeck* and *Lulu* extends the trombone both in range and virtuosity as never before. Much of this writing gives one the impression that it was conceived at the key-board; it seems not to be based on a knowledge of the trombone. It sounds really brilliant in its context, however, and can be played really accurately and well, even if, at first glance, it seems so un-trombonistic as to be impossible.

Recent technical developments

The years immediately after the Second World War saw a complete change of style both of playing and, more important, of equipment used in the trombone sections of British symphony orchestras. Up to this time, the instruments which had been in use for at least half a century generally had a very small bore (.450 in.) with bell sizes of about 6½ in. for the 1st and 2nd trombones, and were supplemented of course, by the traditional G bass trombone. Although in the hands of really fine players these instruments had a not at all unpleasant style, their bad characteristics generally out-weighed their good ones. Their clarity in *pp*, when they blended very well with the small bore trumpets then in use, was probably the only favourable aspect. At loud levels, the sound deteriorated and, save in the hands of the very best players, the sound too often simulated tearing canvas. The favourite makers were Antoine Courtois (Conservatoire model) and Hawkes (later Boosey & Hawkes) (Artists' Perfected).

In America, on the other hand, German and Bohemian influences had always been the strongest in music and except for a few isolated instances of French and Italian influence, the symphony orchestras used German-type trombones which became the basis of the designs adopted by the American manufacturing companies.

The first stage in the revolution in British trombone playing was the acceptance of medium-bore instruments. These had already been used for several decades in dance bands, and although many of them did not have a particularly attractive tone quality they were generally much better instruments than the old small-bore ones, with superior slide action, much smoother legato, and a better range of dynamics. Various medium-bore models by both British and U.S. makers were used, while the G bass trombone was retained as third trombone.

By the mid-50s the new large-bore trombones were coming into use because, I believe, of their great superiority as instruments, not only their broader sound. Nevertheless, the richer sound was very much admired by all who heard it and when the big-toned Bb bass trombone finally ousted the G trombone, British trombone sections began to compare well with those of any other country.

It has been said that British players make German sounds on American instruments. While this is not wholly true, they do tend to make a darker sound than their American counterparts, mainly through using larger mouthpieces.

It might be worth adding that the small F tubas which were used with the small-bore trombones have now all but vanished, having been replaced generally by large-bore band-type EE flat bass tubas. In their turn these were being replaced in the late 1960s by the large-bore CC tubas. Similarly the large-bore French horn sound which has been customary in the U.S.A. for a long time has only recently appeared in Britain. In the interim period there appeared to be two horn or trombone sections in the same orchestra, since at certain dynamics and in the hands of not very good players, the medium-bore horn sounds very much like the large-bore trombone. I can recall hearing a performance by a well-known British orchestra of the Symphony in C by Schubert where the repeated accompanying octaves which alternate between trombone and horns in the first movement sounded exactly the same.

If all this seems a little away from the subject, I make no apology for including it. There are so many differing requirements of style from the modern symphonic trombone section that it is necessary for the player to see these changes in perspective. Other countries will have had their 'revolutions' decades before this; in some cases they are, I believe, yet to come. The modern large-bore trombone has, in my opinion, a much wider range of expression and colour than has ever been thought possible. It can imitate the older styles of the smaller-bore instruments as well as fulfil its own majestic potential, without necessarily detracting from national styles.

Some aspects of orchestral technique

Angle of instrument

This gives the trombone the possibility of achieving an even wider spectrum of tone colour. The level of *fff* can be unimaginably powerful with the bell up—a very useful 'trump card', but one to be treated with the greatest possible respect, and to be used perhaps only in a concert. The A major chord, for example, at the end of Berlioz *Le Carnaval Romain* overture is almost guaranteed to bring the audience to its feet if played in this way by trumpets, cornets, and trombones.

Of more general use is the slight angling down of the bell which serves for the great majority of *f* tutti playing. It is not overpowering and mixes well with the other brass and woodwind. *F* to *mf* with *bells up*—horizontal and with no obstructions, so that the sound really 'gets across'—is quite a different matter. All the richness and fullness of the modern instruments—the ring of the third and fifth overtone partials—can bring about what is surely as beautiful a sound as any to be found in a symphony orchestra. Bells-up *pp* can sound equally fine. Whether playing in a section or individually, the unambiguous clarity of the upper register means that one can play really softly and still carry the sound to the corners of the biggest hall (the 'chorale' section in the last movement of Brahms's 1st Symphony for instance).

Double parts

One problem that the symphony or band trombonist has sometimes to contend with is that of 'double' parts, usually arrangements, where first and second trombone parts are printed on the same page. If the first trombone sits on the right of his section, which is my personal preference, he then has the difficulty of reading at an angle of 45 degrees across an 8 or 9 in. bell, and of seeing the conductor at the same time. Apart from providing needless difficulties, this can in time move the embouchure off-centre, or aggravate this fault if it already exists. I have overcome it by insisting on two copies of such parts, and I always sit on the left of my music-stand. This gives myself and my section also the opportunity to raise or lower the instrument as described already.

Valve-trombone parts

In Italy, the valve trombone (q.v.) was for many years the customary orchestral instrument. Although inferior in everything except mobility to the slide trombone, the instrument was much used by composers of the late nineteenth century, notably Verdi, Mascagni, Leoncavallo, and Puccini. Much of the work of these composers presents little in the way of difficulty to today's slide-trombone players, but some of the operas, notably *Otello* and *Falstaff*, provide good exercises in technical agility, legato tonguing, and flexibility. These parts are difficult, but can, of course, be managed. What is often not realized, however, is that the valve trombone had only about half of the weight of sound of the present-day symphony trombone; parts written for the valve trombone should therefore be played accurately and flexibly, but not too loudly!

Some problems of musicianship in the orchestra

To play the trombone well in tune demands a good ear, and a quick response to changing conditions of intonation, i.e. deciding with whom one has to play in tune! There are many other problems of musicianship, however, which also have to be tackled and solved. The trombone has a powerful voice and it is essential that rhythm, for instance, must be absolutely correct. Everyone hears the trombone. Not everyone can pick out poor intonation, but they can all tell when music is not played together.

I have often been asked 'By how much do you anticipate the conductor's beat?' I invariably answer 'I don't'. Assuming that there is no technical reason why the production should be delayed, and that one is capable of playing at exactly the moment one chooses, then the problem is of not starting too soon! There are very few conductors, in my experience, who want or expect a chord from the orchestra to be precisely *on* the beat. I often regard the time to play as being when the beat stops moving, perhaps above the conductor's head! The time to play can even be a quarter of a second *after* that! It is perfectly possible to conduct with a short precise downward movement, and to expect an orchestra to play at the *bottom* of the beat. From my own experience, however, I know that this can provide a really nasty string sound and sometimes makes ensemble playing very difficult for the winds except in the best orchestras. For this reason, even short chords tend to be shown by conductors in a comparatively lengthy movement. The kind of preparatory twitch also makes it possible for string players to poise their bow arms and start their vibrato, and for brass players to breathe enough air to play what may be a very lound powerful chord.

It should be noted that there are at least two basic methods of conducting in general use. One of these stops the baton movement regularly in 'clicks', the other generally maintains a fairly continuous movement with only slight pulse-indications. The latter is much favoured by symphonic conductors of Germany and central Europe. The Russians tend to be more sparing in movement and more precise in definition, and are generally regarded as having better technical facility for showing the players the required effect, usually without the necessity for any explanation.

Rhythm often presents great difficulties for trombonists. In particular such examples as ♩. ♪ and $\frac{4}{4}$ ♩ ♩ ♩ seem to bring about endless arguments. To me, the cardinal rule is *subdivide*. It is essential for each player to have a silent 'ticker' mechanism in his head. It may be calculated or completely subconscious, but properly applied it will make all rhythms absolutely accurate. In fact what begins as a calculation should very quickly become subconscious. The best musicians can usually do this very well and very naturally.

The ♪♪ rhythm is often distorted into ♩ ♪ or worse ♩ ♪♪ (24th or triplet ♪). In some contexts the sense and intention of the music do not seem compatible with an absolutely accurate ♪♪ in slow time. There is a kind of traditional way of playing this figure for instance in nineteenth-century Italian opera, when a group of 5  seems to approximate most closely to what is generally played. (Benjamin Britten, who must have heard this method of playing often enough, actually wrote it himself in the *War Requiem*.) Although this is a rather elementary problem, it is found often enough in amateurs and students for it to be worth while arranging for two students to work together at the following exercise:

A table top is quite adequate for practice purpose. A little reflection will show that the slow, across-the-beat triplets that I mentioned earlier can be organized quite simply as follows:

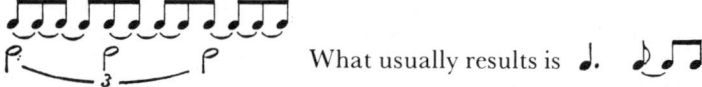 What usually results is

as most players wait for someone else in the brass section to move first!

The distance from the conductor can often lead to the risk of being late. I have already touched on the problem of starting together with the nearer parts of the orchestra. What is often much more difficult is to take up a phrase while others are already playing it. Very often short rests which precede such interjections tend to be elongated, which makes the entry late. The finale of the *Symphonie Fantastique* is a typical example. In the six-eight section, at No. 70, the quaver rest, if carefully observed, will be too long. It is not the production of the next note which takes time, but the intake of breath which most players instinctively make during the rest. There is simply not enough time to do this.

Another persistent problem is the hurrying which almost always comes about when sustained playing is followed by detached notes with rests between them. These rests become progressively shorter and the notes closer together, causing the whole passage to rush, if not to tumble headlong!

A similar situation arises when a trombone or brass section gets 'the bit between its teeth' and stampedes away with a loud running passage when they become more used to the speed at which it goes. A good conductor should never let this happen. If he does he would be well advised not to try to stop it, or glorious confusion can result. Choice of the right speed—right for the players and therefore the piece—is the key to the prevention of this terrifying possibility.

These points may not seem peculiar to the trombone. Indeed one can find them on all instruments. However, playing with an orchestra or band seems always to offer the same problems of rhythm, and, if the reader is aware that they might happen, the chances are that they won't!

Section playing

It is well known that french horns hunt in pairs. It is equally true that trombones sound at their best in a section of at least three. The three members of a regular symphony trombone section have somewhat diverse responsibilities. The first trombone, generally accorded the title of principal or solo trombone, has the responsibility for co-ordinating and, to some extent, organizing the work of his team. Unless he is particularly fortunate, he may well need much diplomacy and tact in order to persuade his colleagues to play in the way he wants. The best method, of course, is by example. The first trombone parts in the symphony orchestra are almost invariably more difficult than the others, even if only because of their greater upward range, and as section leader the first trombone player needs all possible co-operation from his colleagues to help him in his primary function—which is to play his own notes!

The second trombonist needs also to be something of a diplomat, to fill in between first and third, to make a good balance and match the intonation. A full round tone and a good ear are absolutely essential. The bass trombonist, as we have seen, has his own special difficulties of low register, and breath control. He must take care not to drag at all, but at the same time not to lead the section from underneath, or to overbalance when playing in the middle register. He has a special responsibility to fit in and co-operate with the tuba.

The situation of a symphonic trombone section is not so different from that of a string quartet. The members all depend upon each other for a really sensitive, musical rapport. In a good section the first trombone has hardly ever to say a word to 'organize' his team. In a section which may not be so used to playing together, some practice of slow chorale-type music can have extremely beneficial results. I recommend for this Alfred Jacobs' 'Trio Studien' from *Studienwerke für Posaune*. Jacobs, in the simplest possible way, makes the three players listen really carefully, so that their intonation and ensemble can benefit from even a short session together. The scheme is that one of the three parts moves independently while the other two have to play together. By carefully adjusting exact fifths, octaves and thirds, as well as playing his notes in time with one other player, these little studies crystallize the problems of ensemble, that are met in a symphonic trombone section and systematically help to solve them. When one has tried these methods they seem so obviously sensible and practical that one wonders why they have not been thought of before!

The foregoing remarks apply to any section of trombones in any kind of ensemble. Players with a bright, clear sound and good high register naturally graduate to first trombone. Those with perhaps an inferior high register but a good solid sound work best on second—and of course the bass trombone needs an even fuller sound. Each has his own part to play. The feeling of mutual dependability and co-operation leads to a great deal of satisfaction, musical and otherwise, and goes a long way towards making the job of playing in a trombone section a very rewarding one.

Solo playing

It has been said that for a trombonist to perform an extended solo he must be 120 per cent sure of himself. This does not refer to vanity, but rather to a need for careful preparation so that nothing at all is ever left to chance. For most players, concerto playing presents one over-riding problem, even if there is no particular technical barrier: this is, of course, the capacity to 'stay the distance', to finish the piece with the kind of brilliance with which one begins it. Very often one finds the most exacting passages at the end of the concerto.

Solo-playing needs not only good endurance, but also clever tactics. Every solo piece will have 'corners' of great difficulty, and would-be soloists will make sure that they can get round these, by prodigious practice. There are always also 'coasting' sections, where there is neither difficulty nor strain, which can be taken very easily. These, of course, need practice but not the amount of effort concentrated on the difficult 'corners'. Passages of great technical difficulty or physical strain should sometimes be completely omitted in practice of the solo as a whole. They should be practised separately then included in the complete run-through. This ensures that one does not always have to cope with the rest of the piece with a tired lip. One's lip endurance and energy need to be conserved throughout the piece, so that one is never 'all-in' at the end. After all, there may even be an encore!

It has always been a matter of considerable regret to me that there is no classical repertoire of trombone concertos, comparable to the Mozart horn concertos. Perhaps a few baroque ones come nearest to this category, but they offer difficulties of altitude as they were originally written for the alto trombone.

Although the modern concerto repertoire is somewhat limited, it continues to grow. As more composers become aware of the potentialities of the trombone and as the standard of playing generally rises, it is to be hoped that in the future the trombone concerto performance will not be the rarity it is at the moment.

As symphony orchestras demand—and get—stronger, bigger, louder, fuller trombone sounds, the compatibility between this 'heavy' playing and the virtuosity and range needed for the concerto player becomes something of a problem. Ideally, solo performers should use slightly smaller mouthpieces, and possibly instruments also, than those which give the best orchestral sound. I believe it absolutely necessary to play really strongly in concertos, and to use all manner of dynamics, so that every colour in the kaleidoscopic range of the trombone is brought into play. The soloist who just tickles the instrument is not worthy of the name.

A very real practical problem when playing concertos with orchestra is that of orchestral balance. It is essential to point the trombone away from and not *at* the conductor, otherwise in *ff* passages he will have very little idea of what the orchestra is doing!

The trombone is often thought of as a loud instrument—which, of course, it can be. But it can play also much more softly than many conductors believe to be possible, and accompaniments can often be much too loud.

7

VARIOUS INSTRUMENTS

The bass trombone

Historically speaking, the number of different sizes of trombones has gradually been reduced over the centuries, and compared with the descant, alto, tenor, bass, and contrabass trombones available in earlier centuries we have now for all practical purposes only one size of instrument in general use. Of course, alto and G or F bass trombones are still used in certain circles, but the B♭ trombone reigns supreme. The 'tenor' trombone is in fact generally known just as 'trombone'. The bass trombone is however worthy of some separate consideration.

It has an extra-large bore (.562 in.) with a 9 or 10 in. bell, and an F rotary valve, or sometimes even 2 valves to F and E or E♭. It has sometimes been suggested that this is a makeshift instrument, a large-bore tenor trombone, masquerading as a bass trombone. But the quality of sound when played with a very large mouthpiece is a true bass trombone sound—extension and enrichment of the tenor trombone sound in the lower register that is specifically the province of the bass trombone.

The bass trombone, apart from its difference in bore and bell flare (the bell tube expands much sooner on the bass trombone) is very similar to the tenor trombone that we have already discussed in great detail. It has exactly the same characteristics and similar problems; these are tackled in precisely the same way.

The working range of the instrument is:

and most good players can extend this down to pedal C, B, or B♭ and upwards to F. It is, if anything more responsive than the tenor trombone at lower dynamics in all registers, especially is legato, but many bass trombonists find that staccato playing in the middle and low register is very difficult, and cannot match the clarity and ability to play short notes of the tenor trombone in its middle and upper registers.

The study of the bass trombone should proceed exactly as for the tenor trombone. I advocate the study of the *trombone* regardless of whether the student would like to be a high jazz player or a low symphonic bass trombonist. There does come a time, however, when it becomes obvious that a particular student has a real talent for low register playing. He may not be so good at high notes, though I have known some bass trombonists who play equally well in the high and the low registers. Perhaps one very obvious factor should not be overlooked: the vast quantities of air needed when playing the bass trombone loudly in the low register requires a fairly large pair of lungs. Usually large lungs come in large bodies, and perhaps only really king-sized students are best suited to the bass trombone! This does not mean that smaller people cannot cope with the instrument—there are enough 'shortie' bass trombonists to prove this point.

Although a study of the scores of the standard orchestral repertoire will show that the bass trombone descends below the bass clef comparatively rarely, it is on his performance of the F valve register that the bass trombonist tends to be judged. Although it is difficult at first to match the Bb non-valve notes, assiduous practice should make good the difference. Care should be taken not to force the F valve notes, or to distort the embouchure in attempting to overcome the extra resistance which is encountered. Everything remains exactly the same; the only difference should be the extra demand upon the diaphragm, which has to work a little harder, to push air against the greater resistance which the convoluted F tubing offers.

Probably the toughest physical difficulty for the bass trombonist is to play in the register just above the pedal notes, B, C, and C♯. These notes displace a vast volume of air, especially when played loudly, and here lung size and muscular strength really do make a difference. It is not unusual for a young (or even not-so-young) player to find that his head is spinning after a lengthy, loud, low passage. One frequent pitfall is that a player tries to make the air flow too quickly, thus causing a wobbly or shaky sound. It needs a low voltage (flow) and high amperage (volume) at all except very loud levels, when the air seems to disappear after an astonishingly short note. Conservation of air can be a real problem, and the bass trombonist needs to listen carefully to make sure he does not overblow; above a certain degree of loudness, a note starts to become uneven and to 'rasp'—trying to make more sound than the instrument will give really defeats the object.

The bass trombone, which was specified from the time when trombones were first used until the beginning of the twentieth century in parts of Europe and until the 1950s in Britain, was the bass trombone in F (Europe), and which in Great Britain was late in the nineteenth century modified to the bass trombone in G. The G trombone may occasionally be seen in British brass bands. To the non-brass-playing musician the existence of a trombone built in G but playing with B♭ and E♭ instruments must be rather puzzling. A bass trombone in F or E♭ would seem more logical. We are told that these instruments were too heavy and unwieldy to be carried and played when marching. It has been suggested, however—and I am inclined to agree with the idea—that playing tonic and dominant as it usually did—'oom-pah' notes in the favourite march keys of E♭, A♭ or D♭—the slide has to alternate from 7th position to 5th or 3rd, and the spectacle of the extended 7 or 8 feet tube in the front rank of the band (not for nothing was the trombone referred to as the 'kid-shifter' in Northern England) made the G trombone a valuable spectacular asset;—it must have been a fearsome sight! The slide of the G bass trombone is too long for any normal right arm, and it is fitted with a handle to enable the furthest positions to be reached.

The downward range of the G trombone only reached D♭ and left a gap of a diminished fifth above the 'pedal' register. For orchestral use a rotary valve actuating 'D' or 'C' extensions (exactly similar to the B♭ and F in principle) was necessary to play nineteenth century compositions—e.g. by Weber, Brahms, and Strauss—which had been originally conceived for the F bass trombone and which included low C and B.

Most of the world's great instrument makers produce bass trombones (see the list on p. 1). Many of them furnish their instruments with not one valve but two, with the extra semitone (E) or whole-tone E♭ valve fitted to the F valve tubing. Because of the extreme weight of the 2-valve bass trombone, however, many players prefer the model with the optional E valve, which is fitted in the tuning slide of the F section, and can be added as and when required. Still others prefer just to pull out the F tuning slide to E whenever the low B is required. This needs careful practice to memorize the two sets of positions.

A radical solution to bass trombonists' problems in the low register is the 'in line' two-valve system. Gebr. Alexander, the German instrument company originally used this on their F bass trombone, designed for the playing of contrabass trombone parts. In 1971, Boošey & Hawkes of London introduced it on their 'Sovereign' bass trombone, with valves in F and C, and the 'in-line' concept has been since taken up internationally by most leading brass instrument makers. In addition to the usual F valve, a second valve of slightly larger bore tubing gives G (or G♭) in the first position. This may be used in combination with the F valve; together they give E♭ or D. Some players prefer the second valve to be in G♭ because of the fourth position line-up for G (on the B♭ trombone) and C with two valves. Either arrangement makes the 'in-line' valve idea far superior to the old system.

Finally, an ingenious (if somewhat impractical) way around the problem of making a trombone in a lower key, with a slide short enough not to be too cumbersome. In 1910 F.C.Hawkes of the Salvation Army invented a bass trombone in E♭ with two slides. The second slide was in the bell section, and was operated by a system of pulleys so that forward movement of the main slide caused backward movement of the rear slide. This idea falls down only because of the enormous problems of inertia and mechanical efficiency but its ingenuity is to be much admired. The bore of the instrument is however ridiculously small and for this reason the sound is not particularly good. The instrument, which is in a fine state of preservation and still works, is jealously guarded at the Salvation Army museum in London.

For bass trombonists in search of a repertoire for study or solo playing, I recommend Tom Everett's 'Annotated Guide to Bass Trombone Literature'.

The contrabass trombone

This was originally conceived by Richard Wagner for use in *The Ring* and was to have been built in CC with a double slide. There were several models designed and made up to the 1880s. The advent of the large bore B♭ and F and the application of rotary valves to the F bass trombone made this extremely cumbersome instrument, made when narrower bores were the custom and slides were primitive by modern standards, obsolete. A carefully designed BB or CC trombone made by modern manufacturers with well-made and balanced double slides which do not need a rotary change, could revolutionize the lower reaches of the orchestral brass and add another colour to the concert and brass band.

The alto trombone

In orchestral scores written up to the end of the nineteenth century, three different members of the trombone family were usually specified, alto, tenor, and bass, pitched in E♭, B♭, and F respectively. Although until recently only the B♭ was in general use, there has been a revival of interest in the alto trombone in the last decade in Britain and the U.S.A. (In Germany the alto never completely disappeared, and is still often used when specified in the works of classical composers.)

Because of this revival of interest the alto trombone is now often seen in symphony orchestras. First trombone players will be expected to be familiar with it, and we should consider the various aspects of playing it, and its use in the modern symphony orchestra.

Built in the key of E♭, its lowest usable note is A and the high register extends to F

(CONCERT PITCH)

Because of the reduced size of the instrument, the positions are very much closer together, and intonation therefore more critical—a mere ⅛ in. on the slide can make a marked difference.

High notes are a little safer on the alto trombone; they are further apart than on the tenor, being lower in the harmonic series, but they still have to be played, and the alto trombone should not be looked on as an easy way to play high notes.

The bore and bell-size of the alto are, of course, somewhat smaller than the tenor trombone. Thus the sound quality is brighter and clearer. With the increasing use of larger bore tenor trombones and big mouthpieces, the sound quality is often too 'fat' for alto trombone parts, only reaching the right degree of brightness when it is much too loud for a proper balance. This is the real reason for the use of the alto trombone, in my opinion, and its tone colour which blends with the surrounding trumpets, horns, and lower trombones, amply justifies its use. It forms a 'bridge' between the trumpets and trombones.

The study of the alto trombone is more difficult than would be expected. It has to be taken very seriously, and scales, long notes, and studies must be practised assiduously.

Choice of a mouthpiece is probably the biggest problem that one faces. Ideally it should have the same rim as the tenor trombone mouthpiece. It is worth going to the trouble of having a combination mouthpiece made, consisting of a threaded rim with a large underpart for the tenor trombone, and a smaller shallower cup throat and backbore for the alto; but if the player can use two completely different mouthpieces without upsetting his embouchure he is even better off.

In any case, one must find a mouthpiece or underpart which will suit the alto trombone well enough to give a good sound and intonation. Intonation of the harmonic series—1st position notes—is more critical on the alto than on the tenor trombone, and needs even more care in the selection and fitting of a mouthpiece.

Although there is some twentieth-century music which exploits the alto trombone (Britten—*Burning Fiery Furnace*, and *The Building of the House*, Stravinsky—*The Flood*, Berg—*Three Orchestral Pieces*, etc.) most of the repertoire is from the baroque period to the end of the nineteenth century. Of the normal orchestral repertoire, the following works are best suited to the alto trombone:

Mozart—Masses in C and C minor, Requiem, Vespers

Beethoven—Symphonies 5,6,9,*Missa Solemnis*, etc.

Mendelssohn—*Reformation* symphony and *Ruy Blas* overture

The alto trombone enables the player to use the dynamics which are specified by the composer. The underlining effect of the doubling of choral writing by trombones, which was standard practice from the time of Bach, is indeed splendid. Obviously the trombones must not play too loudly, but if properly balanced, the alto trombone in particular can ring out with the alto voices, producing a thrilling effect, and transforming what is often the weakest part of a choral ensemble.

There are alto trombones currently available from several manufacturers. Bach, Yamaha, Selmer (Paris), Courtois, Latzsch, Alexander and Weltklang. Individual preference and price are probably the main factors affecting choice! The Yamaha, apparently an improved version of the Latzsch, probably has the best intonation and sound quality. The Bach and Latzsch have greatest intonation problems and need careful mouthpiece choice and fitting, but the very fine—and very different—sound qualities which each possesses makes this extra care worthwhile.

The valve trombone

The substitution of three piston valves for the trombone slide came about in the middle of the nineteenth century. Berlioz wrote a part for valve trombone in the *Damnation of Faust* and its use was current in military music of the time. Only in Latin countries did it catch on, however, and valve trombones are still to be found in Spain, Portugal, and Italy. The only important effect on orchestral trombone playing was that Verdi and the other Italian opera composers scored for it, providing a few problems for future slide trombone players.

Regarding the instrument itself, nothing very good can be said about it; it has endemic intonation problems, no great dynamic range but all the technical advantages that three valves can give it. However, the modern American version is a wonderful instrument on which to play jazz, and there are some really fine exponents of it. This does not mean that jazz players do not need in-tune instruments, but when one is used to coping with the problems of a three-valve instrument these difficulties are minimized. These problems are very apparent to the player of the slide-trombone who is used always to correct intonation by minute slide corrections. The valve trombonist makes these corrections like a cornettist or other players of valved brass instruments, with tiny unconscious adjustments of the embouchure.

The bass trumpet

Developed from an original idea of Richard Wagner, the bass trumpet very occasionally appears in the symphony orchestra. It is usually played by a trombonist, because of its close affinity of sound, bore, and mouthpiece size. We should consider some of the difficulties which may be encountered by the trombonist when he joins the trumpet section.

Bass trumpets are, for orchestral purposes, traditionally made in C (or Bb) and Eb (or F). C instruments are intended for trombonists, Eb instruments for trumpet players, although a trumpet player is only very occasionally to be found using a bass trumpet in Eb.

Trombonists are rather prone to make the bass trumpet sound like a valve trombone. The difference between the two instruments is, indeed, not very great, and they share the same intonation difficulties that any slide-player inevitably encounters when he uses valves.

For my own part, I agree with the conception of the bass trumpet as a downward continuation of the orchestral trumpet sound, which is a much harder, brighter, narrower sound than that of the modern large-bore symphony trombone. It has a unique sound quality, not to be found on any other instrument, and is always particularly to be noticed in Wagner's *ring* cycle.

Not many trombonists are able to make this trumpet-like quality of tone, and a specially shallow mouthpiece is required. Once heard, however, it makes the rather larger valve-trombone sound seem out of place, in Wagner at any rate.

This latter sound is perhaps of more use in the opening fanfares of the *Sinfonietta* by Janáček, for instance, where a B♭ bass trumpet (or even bass flugelhorn) is more successful. This type of instrument is, of course, invaluable in modern jazz writing, and there are some very fine exponents of it. American instruments all tend to be of the 'compressed valve-trombone' variety, and one needs to go to Europe to find a true bass trumpet.

The main practical problems that face the orchestral trombonist who plays the bass trumpet are those of pitch and transposition, apart from considerations of the actual tone-quality. To get used to a C instrument is much more difficult than would be supposed, and to accustom oneself to Wagner's transpositions can be even more difficult than they would be if one were playing a B♭ instrument. This is usually solved in opera houses by writing out the transpositions for bass trumpet in C. Its range is fairly extensive, and goes up to

E in *Das Rheingold*, and can play down to the
(CONCERT PITCH)

low F♯ or lower, with four valves. A four-valve

instrument is generally to be advised in order to minimize intonation difficulties.

The euphonium

As it usually falls to one of the members of a symphony orchestra trombone section to play what are often important parts for tenor tuba or euphonium, a few words about some problems that may be encountered with it may not be out of place.

In the symphony orchestra the euphonium appears as a tenor tuba, and the extreme kind of vibrato used in the British brass band is regarded as out of place in orchestral surroundings. When played 'straight' or with a minimal vibrato the euphonium has an extraordinarily powerful hall-pervasive quality of sound that is unique in music, and really offers an upward continuation of the tuba range. Of the various makes of instrument available, the British 4-valve Besson, or the Boosey & Hawkes 'Sovereign' and 'Imperial' models are considered to have the fullest, richest sound. They also have an ingenious system of compensating pistons which assists intonation problems. American instruments are generally of smaller bore and very responsive, but produce a timbre of lighter character, and have only a primitive tuning compensation.

The most obvious problem to the trombone player is, of course, intonation. Although he will be able to humour some discrepancies with the embouchure, he will be so used to altering the slide positions that it will take some time for him to learn to depend upon 'lipping' for tuning adjustment. After the straight-through freedom of the trombone, he will also encounter much greater 'resistance' in the euphonium. Except in maximum *ff* this does not mean that it is harder to play, and in fact he can take soft entries with considerably more abandon than he dare in the trombone! Production is however generally required to be heavier in *ff* playing. Finger-technique is not particularly difficult to acquire, but has to be worked at. It is probably easiest to assimilate the special character of the euphonium if the trombonist deserts his trombone for a few weeks, and plays in some kind of concert or brass band in order to cover the many technical facets of the instrument. I have known this give young players a kind of cross-check on their trombone playing; having to tackle similar problems in a different way can shed light on the original problems, and very often solves them.

As the first player in a symphony orchestra section has to deal with alto trombone and probably bass trumpet as well, it is a good idea to let the second player look after the euphonium. He should be able to provide as his normal stock-in-trade the rich, full, warm sound that the euphonium needs. It also gives him an added interest—and probably even financial help too!

The principal works that require a euphonium include:

Strauss – *Don Quixote*
        Ein Heldenleben

Mahler – 7th Symphony (really needs a smaller-bore baritone)
Holst – *The Planets* (strong playing—like a whole section)
Ravel/Mussorgsky – *Pictures at an Exhibition* (solo in 'Bydlo')
Bax – *Overture to a Picaresque Comedy* and 4th Symphony
Havergal Brian – Several symphonies
Janáček – *Sinfonietta* (requires two)
　　　　　　Capriccio (important solo part)
Respighi – *Pines of Rome* (stage band—baritone)

In my opinion it is often a good idea to have ophicleide parts, particularly in Berlioz, played by the euphonium instead of a big orchestral bass tuba. With the best of intentions even when playing all the notes accurately and observing the dynamics meticulously, the composer's idea of balance may be completely wrecked by the overbearing bass tuba sound. This is quite apart from the fact that the extreme high register of the bass tuba cannot always be relied upon, except in the hands of a virtuoso.

The sackbut

In the early 1970s there has been a great deal of research into Medieval, Renaissance, and Baroque music. The sackbut, which was virtually an early trombone, is much more familiar in sound than the simply made yet weird-sounding shawms, racketts, crumhorns, etc. Various makers, mainly in Germany, have produced replicas which are in the author's view only moderately successful. It is perfectly possible, by cutting 3 or 4 inches off the bell, to produce an authentic sounding sackbut from an old small or medium-bore trombone. The resulting sound is very light and gentle, fitting in very well with the tone-quality of the other old instruments. Careful study of the appropriate style in which to play this most interesting 'new' repertoire is needed.

THE TROMBONE IN THE
BRASS BAND

The brass band, as found in Britain and Australasia, has always fascinated me. In a way, it is an anachronism. In many areas, it perpetuates playing styles which are regarded by modern professional players as 'dated', to say the least. There is, however, for all their possible lack of sophistication and their careful cultivation of their own traditional styles, a vigour and enthusiasm about these amateur players that would put many professionals to shame.

Brass band trombones do not usually play as continuously as, for instance, euphoniums and cornets and are used in not too dissimilar a way to the trombones in the orchestra—to make an occasional change of tone colour, and add emphasis, as well as to function occasionally as a solo voice. Brass bands normally employ three trombones, two tenor and one bass. Traditionally small-bore tenors and G bass have been the rule, but in recent years these have often been replaced by medium-bore tenors and large bore Bb and F bass.

The old 'pea-shooter' small-bore trombone has always been an extremely difficult instrument to play well, and has an alarming tendency to over-blow or 'rip'. When this happens the real trombone qualities of nobility of sound, with just enough 'edge' for projection, are lost. The 'circular saw' quality of the over-blown small-bore trombone can easily predominate and make this the most often heard trombone sound. The answer is to limit volume and use a deeper mouthpiece—assuming that there are no embouchure problems.

The medium-bore trombone will tend to eliminate much of this traditional aspect of trombone sound, and should give a much wider range of dynamics.

Band trombonists frequently have great dexterity and brilliance, and some of the best players in championship bands are very good indeed—many have taken the trouble to study with professionals and have a well-organized technique and good sound quality. Unfortunately, however, many bandsman-trombonists still perpetuate the faults of 'smile' embouchure, note stopping with tongue, tongue penetration, and so on, that have already been discussed within these pages. In many bands the trombone, possibly because it is more difficult, is not played as well as the other instruments—perhaps the faults I have mentioned are more evident on the trombone. Many such players are out of touch with modern professional standards and would be astounded at the technical levels that have been reached.

The method of scoring for brass band is to use the treble clef for all instruments (except the bass trombone). One can see the sense in this—one basic clef reduces the amount of theoretical knowledge needed and makes the transfer of a player from one instrument to another comparatively easy. For the trombonist, however, it is very limiting. In all other fields the trombone is not treated as a transposing instrument. Learning bass and tenor (even alto!) clefs not only gives the band trombonist unlimited scope for playing with other combinations of instruments, but makes available vast quantities of study material and solos. It would be fair to say that the bandsman who learns the trombone only as a transposing Bb treble clef instrument needs to free himself from the shackles of the treble clef if he is to make any headway as a trombonist (see chapter on clefs).

Choice of equipment is important, of course, and even if he is unable to afford a really good trombone, then a well-designed mouthpiece will probably help him.

Band trombonists should aim at a big, solid, well-centred straight (vibrato-free) sound in all 'tutti' playing, with no more tongue-application than is necessary for clean production, good breath support and no 'tail' at the end of the note. In solo playing, a really well organized legato, with a 'vocalistic' vibrato. In dynamics, a louder *ff* (with good sound quality to maximum level) and a softer *pp* level.

With all the faults that may be found therein, the brass band remains the best place for young players (in brass band countries, that is) to learn to play and to develop the necessary embouchure strength and reading ability. It has the additional advantage that players in it have often to play 'tunes' and easily acquire the basic musicianship needed to play an expressive melodic line. It is unfortunate that amateur orchestras, in Britain at any rate, are generally of a low standard—I am sure that it is better to play in even a second-rate band than to count rests in a third-rate orchestra!

The trombone in the brass ensemble

Perhaps the best way for interested and otherwise frustrated brass players to express themselves musically is to form themselves into a small brass ensemble, where they may find considerable musical enjoyment and fulfilment.

The standard brass quintet of two trumpets, horn, trombone, and tuba, gives a fine, well balanced sound with marvellous possibilities of musical expression. There is a growing repertoire for this combination of original twentieth-century music which, although sometimes extremely difficult, is well worth playing. Music from the baroque period also arranges well, although in my opinion it sounds better on trumpets and trombones. The trombone suffers slightly in the brass quintet, because of the obvious disadvantage that the slide can never be quite as nimble as valves. However, trombonists can meet this challenge and cope with well-written trombone parts so that they do not appear at a disadvantage. Small ensembles like the brass quintet do offer opportunities of musical expression to trombonists that bigger groups often deny. It is to be hoped that the brass quintet becomes as much a part of musical life as a string quartet—it has an immediate attraction to the listener and will appeal to a much wider public than the somewhat staid vehicles of more conventional chamber music.

The trombone in the concert band

Although the symphonic-type concert-band is virtually unknown in Britain, where brass and 'military' (a smaller concert-band) bands flourish, it does exist in many other musically more enlightened parts of the world, notably the U.S.A. and a few words about the place of the trombone in it are necessary here. In the concert-band the trombone section should function exactly as in a symphony orchestra and should ideally use the same kind of equipment. Although the kind of sound quality that the strings can make in the symphony orchestra is lacking in the concert-band, and therefore the lower *ppp* range of dynamics is hardly ever needed, there are enough colours in the palette of the concert band to give the trombones full rein to their range of dynamics. By careful use of every aspect of technique and expression the trombone section makes a very useful contribution to this kind of 'wind-orchestra'.

Trombone choirs

'Trombone choirs' consisting of multiples of four parts from as few as eight to as many as 40 players are now becoming very popular in the larger music colleges. The sound that such groups produce is unexpectedly beautiful, and much music has been either arranged, or specially written, for them.

9
TEACHING AND LEARNING

Teaching methods

Although there may be exceptions, I strongly believe that instrumental teachers must be really fine players, and able to demonstrate practically what they are teaching. To be able to *describe*, with however fine a mastery of words—metaphor, simile, and imagery—is no substitute for *doing*. The student's conception of clear, rich, broad, liquid, resonant, dark, brilliant, etc., may never match that of his teacher. It is always easier to offer negative criticism—to be constructive one must offer a direct example of what is required. Far from being a poor substitute for playing ability, teaching should be a valuable and ever-increasing adjunct to it. By communicating his enthusiasm and enjoyment of playing to the student, the teacher can give more than knowledge; he can, by his example, pass on the enthusiasm and dedication which will ensure the raising and improvement of playing standards, however high they may appear to be at the present time.

Every student that one meets has some good and some bad points to his playing. Some may find high or low notes, or technical passages, or legato easier than something else. I have found it most beneficial to work at those aspects of playing which a student can do well. This, in my experience, very often improves other areas of his playing. I do not mean that problems should be ignored—far from it—but it is most unrewarding and destructive of a student's security if some special difficulty is relentlessly pursued to the exclusion of all else.

Physical exercise

Any body-building exercise or sport which will tone up and maintain one's general physique and health is worth encouraging. Swimming, particularly underwater, gives added lung capacity and strengthens the whole physique. Ball games in general require a high degree of concentration and co-ordination; these two factors are needed constantly in brass playing, and healthy exercise can only be of help. I would, however, warn against the possibility of serious accident in games where a very hard ball is used, such as cricket or baseball. I have known several very promising young players whose careers have been abruptly terminated, or seriously impaired over a long period, by being struck in the face by one of these projectiles. My advice is to stick to games where there is little or no risk of this happening—and there are plenty to choose from.

Errors and remedies

For convenience I add a summary of the most frequently encountered problems, and suggested remedies. (These remedies should be undertaken with the co-operation of a good teacher.)

(1) *Smile-and-press embouchure* causes hard, unpleasant, nasal sound in middle and low register, some degree of accuracy in high register, but poor sound and tendency to sharpness.

Remedy. Restrict playing temporarily to middle and low register, not above middle B♭, work on middle F with embouchure more open than usual, and with the mouth-corners pointed down, instead of up (this is hard at first, but persevere!). Now, opening the mouth, gradually push forward the lower lip. The middle F will gradually flatten until it eventually falls to the low B♭. As this lumpy slur takes place, push the entire jaw structure forward, until the low B♭ sounds really rich and full. Slow undulations between the two notes should follow, then the whole process should move to the next harmonic series—A then A♭; then continue the process of slurring down, using the bottom lip in a definite forward movement, and keeping the corners of the mouth down, maintaining absolute stillness on the sides of the face. The biggest improvements will already be noticed, sound quality will be improved and will gradually spread to the low register, then gradually upwards. The temptation to stretch the lips must be resisted. The upper register will improve by retracting the bottom lip very slightly. (There is a temporary measure as explained in the chapter on embouchure. Careful practice of all these suggestions will bring about an all-round improvement in sound range and flexibility.)

(2) *Excessive pressure* causes limited endurance, soreness, and swelling or bruising, poor low register, and difficulty in the high register (often in combination with (1)).

Remedy is as for (1), and also long-note practice with a conscious effort to remove mouthpiece from lips. In the high register, where one is most inclined to use heavy pressure, I suggest practising a chromatic sequence of long notes with minimum pressure, and with crescendo-diminuendo on each one. Starting on D above middle C, a sequence of 5 notes in semitones to F sharp and back to D, followed by similar sequences on E♭, E, F, F sharp, G, and so on, upwards, using minimum pressure throughout.

(3) *Tongue penetration* causes over-emphasis in starting a note, tendency to split notes, unreliable high register and difficulty in *pp* production.

Remedy. First practise production without tongue or emphasis, then find the best tongue-seal position for each note, and standardize this position for all types of articulation, as described in the section on production.

(4) *Stopping with tongue* causes unmusical emphasis on note-endings, over-heavy staccato, pre-selection of each new note, and makes smooth legato or tenuto impossible.

Remedy. Check (3) then make sure that the end of each note finishes by closing the glottis, and with the tongue in the middle of the mouth.

(5) *Jaw and lower lip not projected* causes poor low register, stuffy tone quality from the middle register downwards, poor slurring response and makes movement into pedal register difficult. Some players, especially bass trombonists, may try to compensate for lack of jaw-projection by puffing out their cheeks. This is dangerous because it sometimes appears to work and gives a kind of fullness to the lower

register, but without the necessary movement of the lower jaw. Flexibility is never very good and the sound is inferior—quite apart from the unpleasant look of the thing.

Remedy is as for (1) with intensive practice of low register and slurring exercises in and out of pedal register.

(6) '*Bottling-up of air*' behind the tongue before production of note causes explosive, uncontrolled production, and a justified lack of confidence in all dynamics except *mf* and upwards.

Remedy. Make every production a continuous process, from the first intake of breath to the end of the note. The air should never stop moving—either in or out.

(7) *Too much flexibility in right wrist* generally causes uncontrolled intonation and lack of slide precision, speed, and co-ordination, because of wasted movement and time.

Remedy. Turn wrist until thumb and fingers are roughly in the same plane on the trombone slide. Minimize wrist movement, but keep slide hand and wrist supple enough not to jerk the slide.

(8) *Shallow breathing* causes poor phrasing, poor sound quality, lack of accent, lack of slurring power, and poor high register.

Remedy. Conscious use of diaphragm, three-stage breathing, and deep breathing lung-expansion to increase lung capacity, and hence breath support.

(9) *Lack of awareness of glottis valve* causes tight, restricted sound when it is too closed, and lack of control in extreme *pp* levels when permanently open.

Remedy. Simple exercises to familiarize the glottal action —yawning to open, whispering to close; practise diminuendo to silence, closing glottis. Use of practice mute (see p.75) to make throat opening automatic.

(10) *Settling and swelling on notes* causes egg- or pear-shaped notes and makes a true legato and sostenuto impossible.

Remedy. An awareness of actually doing this—careful consideration and practice of (3), and trying to play equal, level notes.

Every student is different—physically, mentally, musically—

and it is therefore impossible to standardize a teaching programme which will suit every individual.

I always try to work at each student's separate pace, and to modify whatever is suggested for each year's work to suit the individual student. I find that by the third year of study they have, save in exceptional cases, reached about the same level. It is, because of the inevitable differences in student abilities which I have outlined, important not to try to standardize their playing. It is, of course, always a pleasant compliment to a teacher when his students try to play exactly like him. However much they try, they are not likely to be carbon copies, and their own personalities eventually assert themselves in their playing. Although similar in many ways, and with a similar assured technique, they eventually emerge as individuals. It is, after all, only when all the technical barriers to artistry are down that true artistry can emerge. This I have always found to be a complete picture of the artist—his personality and character are revealed—he literally bares his soul to a discerning public whenever he plays.

It is, of course, perfectly possible for a student to study by himself as an individual taking lessons from a good teacher. There are, however, as on every instrument, inestimable benefits to be derived from studying in a group; a competitive spirit arises when several people are trying to do the same things at the same time. From any group of, say a dozen or so students, there is always (at least) one of them, who is so conspicuously better at one aspect of playing, however small, that all the others should see it and try to copy. It may be just turning over music or putting in mutes, but each student may do one thing better than his fellows. Of course such fine skills as a clean production, good high or low register, or a smooth legato are sufficiently self-evident; perhaps less evident skills need pointing out. I have known just one outstanding student in a music college trombone group improve all the others enormously simply by his presence.

Apart from these benefits of working with other students, it is as well to point out that there are so many aspects of musicianship and allied studies that are beyond the scope of an instrumental teacher. To be a complete player, the student needs a thorough study of many other aspects of music, apart from the relatively narrow one of playing the trombone. I believe that special emphasis should be placed upon ear-training with care given to rhythmic studies as well as pitch. A good knowledge of harmony, orchestration, and/or band arranging is absolutely essential.

Complete change of embouchure

My advice is often sought by players who feel that, in some way, they are using a 'wrong' embouchure, and want to change it. This whole subject is somewhat delicate, and should be approached with great caution. It has sometimes been necessary for me to alter a 'smile and press' method to a 'pucker-with-corners-down' structure. Although this *can* be done, it is extremely difficult and frustrating both for teacher and student; for a time the student may sound worse than ever, before the 'new' muscles start to work properly. In order to keep one aspect of the embouchure 'feel' common to both methods, I insist that the top lip should make contact with the mouthpiece in the same way as before, even if the mouthpiece seems much too low on the top lip. Very often it will 'ride up' naturally to the best position for the individual student.

If an otherwise orthodox player wishes to move his top lip position on the mouthpiece, possibly to give him greater flexibility, then plenty of flexibility exercises over the entire range of the instrument will, in all probability, accomplish this change in mouthpiece placement quite naturally and gradually. The danger of too drastic a change is that the student may easily over-do some other aspect of his muscular effort to try to make his playing come back to life after a sudden change of mouthpiece placement has temporarily wrecked it. Providing that all other aspects of the embouchure structure are working properly, the best possible position for the lips on the mouthpiece is so conspicuously better than any other that it should be found both naturally and easily.

10
ADVICE TO CONDUCTORS

I find it impossible to resist the temptation to include a few words directed at any conductors or potential conductors who may seek to widen their knowledge of the trombone by browsing through this little book.

Already such a reader will have realized that there is actually more to playing the trombone than he may have thought. Let him, then, realize some of his trombonists' special problems, so that he can help his own performance by improving theirs.

(1) *Distance.* Make your beat clear and distinct to the most distant players. As these will probably include the trombones, make a point of ensuring that they are not placed further away than is absolutely necessary. Never tolerate 'late' playing, for there is absolutely no need for it. The average distance from the conductor's desk to the back of the orchestra can cause a time lag of approximately ♪ in a ♩=120 allegro. If the beat is clear enough, the trombones will play on that point of it which makes for the best ensemble. If this is not so, then make sure that the moment in time when *you* want to hear the sound is made apparent to the heavy brass by some kind of visual indication. In other words, conduct *for* them, and breathe with them.

(2) *High register.* No trombonist can be expected to play indefinitely in the upper register (above high F)

 Do not insist on repetition of tiring passages. If

a trombonist (or any other brass player) fluffs or splits a high note *do not* make your displeasure obvious. He knew before you did, and his own misery is ten times greater than yours. Do not add to it.

(3) *Rehearsal plan.* Have the courtesy to announce the order in which you intend to rehearse well in advance. If possible arrange your rehearsal order so that the greatest number of players can be used at the end of the rehearsal which suits them best. *Do not* keep a brass section twiddling their thumbs in movements in which they do not play, just so that you will not have to wait perhaps a minute or so when you *do* need them. A musicianly trombone and/or trumpet section will almost certainly do some ensemble work together or at the very least some warm-up exercises. If they are expected to sit waiting to play without the chance to do these things, results less than the best may be expected.

Conductors have often complained that the brass section is playing too strongly at a final rehearsal. What usually happens is that the strings and woodwind of a symphony orchestra tend to take it easy at such a rehearsal. They have a fairly continuous effort to make and need to conserve their strength and energy. While this can also apply to the brass, they have a special need to play in exactly the same way as they do in performance, so that phrasing, breathing, and lip-control can be arranged properly. These same conductors who complain of too much volume at the dress rehearsal also call for more and more sound at the performance.

Cherish your trombone section. They can do more to bring an audience to their feet at the end of a performance than an entire string section! Of course, they do not need much encouragement to play loudly; what they do need, however, is sympathetic consideration and help. Even a cursory knowledge of what they have to contend with—possibly gained through reading these pages—may result in better mutual respect and co-operation.

APPENDIX I

Recommended tutors and study material

Many trombone tutors of one sort or another are available, particularly in America. Some are very good, others not so good. The following I personally have used and recommend.

André Lafosse	Méthode Complète (2 vols Leduc)
André Lafosse	Bach Cello Suites (transcribed Leduc)
Muller	Trombone Tutor (Zimm)
Max Schlossberg	Daily Drills and Technical Studies (Baron)
C.Kopprasch	60 Studies (Fischer)
V.Blazhevich	26 Sequences (MCA)
V.Blazhevich	Clef Studies (MCA)
Otto Langey	Practical Tutor (B & H)
George Maxted	20 Studies (B & H)
Rochut	Melodious Etudes (Fischer)
H.W.Tyrell	40 Progressive Studies (B & H)

Worth mentioning as study material, although not strictly speaking a tutor, is the excellent book *The Art of Trombone Playing* by Edward Kleinhammer (Summy-Birchard) in which every aspect of the trombone is thoroughly discussed.

For students of avant-garde technique, Stuart Dempster's *The Modern Trombone* (UCa) is absolutely indispensable, and Buddy Baker's jazz improvisation texts are also highly recommended.

Also recommended are *The Trumpet and the Trombone* by Philip Bate (Ernest Benn) and *The Trombone* by Robin Gregory (Faber).

Abbreviations

picc.	piccolo	cont.	continuo
fl.	flute	strgs.	strings

ob.	oboe	bar.	euphonium
cl.	clarinet	timp.	timpani
bn.	bassoon	perc.	percussion
hn.	french horn	tack-pf.	prepared piano
tpt.	trumpet	xylo.	xylophone
cnt.	cornet	hp.	harp
tmb.	trombone	orch.	orchestra
tba.	tuba	vln.	violin
sax.	saxophone	vla.	viola
pf.	pianoforte	vc.	violoncello
org.	organ	db.	double bass
hpd.	harpsichord		

New material for trombones is constantly appearing. To update the repertoire list on a regular basis would be an impossible task. In order to keep up with the newest ideas and music available, I would recommend the enthusiastic trombonist to become a member of the International Trombone Association, whose secretary is:

> Vern Kagarice
> School of Music
> University of North Texas
> Denton
> TX 76203, USA

For British trombonists, the British Trombone Society similarly offers much to interest them. Both groups publish quarterly magazines. Most top professionals on both sides of the Atlantic give their support and annual conferences are always well attended. The BTS address is:

> 4 Sutton Parade
> Church Road
> London NW4 1RR

APPENDIX II
KEY TO PUBLISHERS

Ac ACCURA MUSIC Box 887, Athens, Ohio 45701

Ahn AHN & SIMROCK Berlin, Germany

Am AMPHION EDITIONS MUSICALES 5, rue Jean Ferrandi, Paris VI, France

Ande EDITION ANDEL UITGAVE Madeliefjeslann, B–8400 Oostende, Belgium

As ASSOCIATED MUSIC PUBLISHERS 866 Third Ave., New York, New York 10022

BA BARENREITER VERLAG Postfach 100329, D–3500 Kassel, Germany

Bara PAOLO BARATTO Wiesenstrasse 4, CH–8008 Zurich, Switzerland

Bel BELWIN-MILLS MUSIC LTD. 250 Purley Way, Croydon CR9 4QD, England

   BELWIN-MILLS Melville, New York 11746

Bela M.P.BELAIEFF Frankfurt, Germany

Benj ANTON J.BENJAMIN Hamburg, Germany

BenP CLAUDE BENNY PRESS 1401 State Street, Emporia, Kansas 66801

BH-W BREITKOPF & HAERTEL Burgstrasse 6, Wiesbaden 1214, West Germany

British agents: ALFRED A.KALMUS LTD. 2–3 Fareham St., London W1V 4DV, England

Bill EDITIONS BILLAUDOT 14 rue de l'Echiquier, Paris X, France

BIM EDITIONS BIM rue du Moleson 14, CH–1630 Bulle, Switzerland

Bone BONESTEEL MUSIC COMPANY Box 845, Youngstown, Ohio 44501

Boo BOOSEY & HAWKES MUSIC PUBLISHERS LTD. 295 Regent St., London W1R 8JH, England

BOOSEY & HAWKES INC. Box 130, Oceanside, New York 11572

Boss BOSSE EDITION Regensburg, Germany

Bosw BOSWORTH et CIE. 45 rue de Ruysbroeck, Brussels, Belgium

Bote BOTE and BOCK K.G. Hardenbergstrasse 9a, 1 Berlin 12, Germany

Bour BOURNE COMPANY 1212 Avenue of the Americas, New York, New York 10036

Bran HAROLD BRANCH PUBLICATIONS 95 Eads St., W.Babylon, New York 11704

BroB   BROUDE BROS. 56 W.45th St., New York, N.Y. 10036

Brog   EDITIONS MUSICALES BROGNEAUX 73 avenue Paul Janson, Brussels, Belgium

BrP   THE BRASS PRESS 136 8th Avenue North, Nashville, Tenn. 37203

Busc   HANS BUSCH MUSIKFORLAG Stubbstigen 3, Lidingo S–181 46, Sweden

Car   CARISCH EDIZIONI MUSICALI Via Gen. Fara 39, 20124 Milano, Italy

CBDM   CeBeDeM (Centre Belge de Documentation Mus) 3 rue du Commerce, Brussels, Belgium

CFG   CFG PUBLISHING COMPANY Box 26, Cold Spring Harbor, New York 11724

Cho   EDITIONS CHOUDENS 38 rue Jean-Mermoz, 75008 Paris, France

Cir   CIRONE PUBLICATIONS Box 612, Menlo Park, Calif. 94025

Col   CHARLES COLIN 315 West 53rd Street, New York, N.Y. 10019

Cole   M.M.COLE PUBLISHING CO. Playboy Building Suite 1602, 919 N. Michigan Ave., Chicago, Ill. 60611

Cosc   SILVIO COSCIA See King

Del   GEORGES DELRIEU & CIE. Nice, France

Deut   DEUTSCHER VERLAG fur MUSIK Karlstrasse 10, 701 Leipzig, East Germany

Dob   LUDWIG DOBLINGER K.G. Dorotheergasse 10, Wien 1, Austria

Don   DONEMUS 51 Jacob Obrechstraat, Amsterdam, Holland

Dor   DORABET MUSIC COMPANY P.O.Box 4124, Hollywood, Calif. 90028

Dur   EDITIONS DURAND & CIE. 4, Place de la Madeleine, Paris, France

EdFa   EDITION FAZER Box 10260, Helsinki 10, Finland

EdMB   EDITIO MUSICA BUDAPEST Hungary

EdMo   EDITION MODERN Franz Joseph Strasse 2, D–8000 Muenchen 40, West Germany

EdMT   EDITIONS MUSICALES TRANSATLANTIQUES 14, Avenue Hoche, 75008 Paris, France

EdPh   EDITIONS PHILIPPO 24, Blvd. Poissonnière, 75009 Paris, France

Em   EMERSON EDITION Ampleforth, Yorks YO6 4HF, England

Ens   ENSEMBLE PUBLICATIONS Box 98, Buffalo, N.Y. 14222

Esc   EDITIONS MAX ESCHIG 48 rue de Rome, 75008 Paris, France

Eul   EDITION EULENBURG Zurich, Switzerland

Euro   EUROPEAN AMERICAN MUSIC CORP. 195 Allwood Rd., Clifton, N.J. 07012

Fab   FABER MUSIC LTD. 3 Queen Square, London WC1N 3AU, England

Fau   RANDALL FAUST Box 2455, Winchester, Va. 22601

Fem   FEMA MUSIC PUBLICATIONS Box 395, Naperville, Illinois 60540

Fet   DAVID FETTER 2819 St. Paul Street, Baltimore, Md. 21218

116   TROMBONE TECHNIQUE

Fisc   CARL FISCHER INC. 62 Cooper Square, New York, N.Y. 10003
Fitz   Y.T.FITZSIMONS COMPANY 615 N.LaSalle St., Chicago, Illinois
        60610
Fog   DAN FOG Graabrodretorv 7, Copenhagen DK 1154, Denmark
Fox   SAM FOX MUSIC SALES CORP. 170 N.E.32nd St., Ft. Lauderdale,
        Fla. 33334
FrP   FREDONIA PRESS 3947 Fredonia Drive, Hollywood, CA 90068
Gal   GALAXY MUSIC CORP. 2121 Broadway, New York, N.Y. 10023
Gehr   CARL GEHRMANS MUSIKFORLAG Box 505, S101 26 Stockholm,
        Sweden
Gen   GENERAL MUSIC PUBLISHING CO. 116 Boylston Street, Boston,
        Mass. 02116
Ger   MUSIKVERLAGE HANS GERIG Drususgasse 7–11, 5000 Koeln,
        Germany
Gerv   GERVAN EDITION MUSICALE 352, Avenue de la Couronne,
        Brussels, Belgium
Glo   GLOUCHESTER PRESS Box 1044, Fairmont, W.Va. 26554
Gras   EDITIONS GRAS 36, rue Pope Charpentier, LaFleche, France
Gro   MUSIKVERLAG GROSCH Lisztstrasse 18, 8000 Muenchen 80,
        Germany
HanW   WILHELM HANSEN MUSIKFORLAG Gothersgade 9–11, 1123
        Copenhagen K. Denmark
Helb   EDITION HELBLING Volketswil-Zurich, Switzerland
Henn   EDITIONS HENN 8, rue de Hesse, 1211 Geneva, Switzerland
Heu   HEUGEL et CIE. Au Menestral 2 bis, rue Vivienne, Paris, France
Hin   HINRICHSEN EDITION 10–12 Baches St., London N1 6DN,
        England
HofL   VEB FRIEDRICH HOFMEISTER–LEIPZIG Karlstrasse 10, 701
        Leipzig, East Germany
Ins   THE INSTRUMENTALIST 1418 Lake Street, Evanston, Illinois
        60204
Int   INTERNATIONAL MUSIC COMPANY 545 Fifth Avenue, New
        York, New York 10017
Is   ISRAELI MUSIC PUBLICATIONS Box 6011, Tel-Aviv, Israel
IsM   ISRAEL MUSIC INSTITUTE Box 11253, Tel-Aviv, Israel
Jer   JERONA MUSIC CORP. 14 Porter Street, Hackensack, N.J. 07601
Job   SOCIETE DES EDITIONS JOBERT 44, rue de Colisee, Paris,
        France
KaWe   EDITION KA WE Brederodestraat, 90 1054 VE Amsterdam,
        Holland
Ken   KENDOR MUSIC COMPANY Delevan, N.Y. 14042
King   ROBERT KING MUSIC COMPANY 112A Main Street, North
        Easton, Mass. 02356
Kjos   NEIL A.KHOS MUSIC CO. 4382 Jutland Drive, San Diego, Calif.
        92117

KSM   KSM PUBLISHING CO. Box 3819, Dallas, Texas 75208

Led   ALPHONSE LEDUC EDITIONS MUSICALES 175, rue Saint Honore, 75001 Paris, France

Lee   NORMAN LEE PUBLISHING CO. Box 2733, Wichita, Kansas 67201

Lem   HENRI LEMOINE et CIE 17, rue Pigalle, Paris, France

Leu   VERLAG F.E.C.LEUCKART Munich, Germany

Lud   LUDWIG MUSIC PUBLISHING CO. 557 East 140th St., Cleveland, Ohio 44110

Mar   ROBERT MARTIN EDITIONS MUSICALES 106 Grande-rue de la Coupee, 71009 Macon, France

Marg   MARGUN MUSIC INC. 167 Dudley Rd., Newton Centre, Mass. 02159

Mau   J.MAURER EDITIONS MUSICALES 7, avenue du Verseau, Woluwe St.Lambert, Brussels 1200, Belgium

McM   McGINNIS & MARX c/o Pietro Deiro 133 7th Avenue, New York, New York 10014

Med   MEDIA PRESS Box 895, Champaign, Illinois 61820

Mers   VERLAG MERSEBERGER Berlin, Germany

Met   EDITIONS METROPOLIS 24, Frankrijklei, Antwerpen, Belgium

MGP   MGP 10 Clifton Terrace, Winchester, Hants., England

Moes   MOESELER VERLAG Wolfenbuettel, Germany

Mole   UITGAVE MOLENAAR N.V.Wormerveer, Holland

MusH   MUSIKK-HUSET A/S Postboks 1459, Vika, Oslo, Norway

MusR   MUSICA RARA Le Traversier, Chemin de la Buire 84170 Monteux, France

MusW   THE MUSIC WORKSHOP RR#2, Box 563 Wolfville, N.S., Canada BOP 1XO

Noga   NOGA MUSIC Box 4025, Jerusalem, Israel

Nordi   AB NORDISKA MUSIKFORLAGET Box 745, 101 30 Stockholm 1, Sweden

Nov   NOVELLO & CO., LTD. 8 Lower James St., London W1R 4DN, England

Om   OMEGA MUSIC CO. 353 E. 52nd Street, New York, N.Y. 10022

Op   OPUS MUSIC PUBLISHERS 1880 Holste Road, Northbrook, Illinois 60062

OR-T   OR-TAV MUSIC PUBLICATIONS 17 Bar Ilan St., Tel-Aviv, Israel

Os   PETE OSTERHOUDT Box 2231, Durango, Colo. 81301

Oxf   OXFORD UNIVERSITY PRESS 16–00 Pollitt Drive, Fairlawn, N.J. 07410

Walton Street, Oxford OX2 6DP, England

Pan   PANTON Prague, Czechoslavakia

Pat   PATERSON'S PUBLICATIONS 38 Wigmore Street, London W1H OEX, England

Pete   C.F.PETERS CORP. 373 Park Ave., South, New York, N.Y. 10016

Ph   PHILHARMUSICA CORP. 110 W.Crooked Hill Rd., Pearl River, NY 10965

Pol   ARS POLANA Karkowskie Przedmiescie #7, 00–068 Warszawa, Poland

Pr   THEODORE PRESSER COMPANY Presser Place, Bryn Mawr, PA 19010

ProA   PRO ART PUBLICATIONS Melville, N.Y. 11746

Ram   BASIL RAMSEY 604 Rayleigh Road, Eastwood, Essex SS9 5HU, England

RicP   EDITIONS RICORDI 3, rue Roquepine, Paris, France

Rid   EDITIONS RIDEAU ROUGE 24, rue de Longchamp, Paris 16, France

Ros   ROSEHILL MUSIC PUBLISHING CO., LTD. The Old House, 64 London End, Beaconsfield, Bucks, HP9 2JD, England

Rub   RUBANK, INC. 16215 N.W.15th Ave., Miami, Fla. 33169

Sal   EDITIONS SALABERT 575 Madison Ave., New York, N.Y. 10022

Sam   SAMFUNDET til udgivelse af DANSK MUSIK Valkendorfsgade 3, DK–1151 Kobenhavn K, Denmark

Sche   SCHERZANDO EDITIONS MUSICALES 14, rue Auguste Orts, Brussels, Belgium

SchG   G.SCHIRMER LTD. Kern House, 61–62 Lincoln's Inn Fields, London WC2A 3XB, England

G.SCHIRMER INC. 866 3rd Ave., New York, N.Y. 10022

SchL   SCHOTT & CO.LTD 48, Great Marlborough St., London W1V 2BN, England

Schul   BLASMUSIKVERLAG FRITZ SCHULTZ Am Maerzengraben 6, 7800 Frieburg-Tiengen, Germany

See   SEESAW MUSIC CORP. 2067 Broadway, New York, NY 10023

Sha   SHAWNEE PRESS Delaware Water Gap, Pa. 18327

Sid   SIDEMTON VERLAG Koln, Germany

Siko   MUSIKVERLAGE HANS SIKORSKI Hamburg, Germany

Sm   SMITH PUBLICATIONS 2617 Gwynndale Ave., Baltimore, Md. 21207

SoNY   SOUTHERN MUSIC PUBLISHING CO. 1740 Broadway, New York, N.Y. 10019

SOUTHERN MUSIC PUBLISHING CO.LTD. 8 Denmark St., London WC2H 8LT, England

SouT   SOUTHERN MUSIC CO. Box 329, San Antonio, Texas 78292

Spr   SPRATT MUSIC PUBLISHER 170 N.E.33rd St., Ft.Lauderdale, Fla. 33334

StPR   STUDIO P/R 224 South Lebanon Street, Lebanon, Ind. 46052

Stu   STUDIO MUSIC CO. 89 Vicarage Road, London, England

Syn   SYNTHESIS PUBLICATIONS 100 West Huston St., New York, N.Y. 10012

Tem   TEMPO MUSIC PUBLICATIONS Box 392, Chicago, Illinois 60690
Tez   MARK TEZAK Weissenburgstrasse, 57, 5 Koln, West Germany
Tou   A TOUCH OF BRASS PUBLISHING 208 W.6th St., N.Vancouver,
   B.C., Canada V7M 1K6
UE   UNIVERSAL EDITION (London) LTD. 2–3 Fareham St., Dean St.,
   London W1V 4DV, England
UNIVERSAL EDITION Vienna, Austria
Uni   UNIVERSE PUBLISHING 733 E 840 North Circle, Orem, Utah
   84057
War   WARNER BROS.MUSIC LTD. 17 Berners St., London W1P 3DD,
   England
WARNER BROS.MUSIC 265 Secaucus Road, Secaucus, N.J. 07094
Wei   JOSEF WEINBERGER 12–14 Mortimer St., London W1N 8EL,
   England
Wein   WEINTRAUB MUSIC COMPANY 33 West 60th St., New York,
   N.Y. 10023
Whal   WHALING MUSIC PUBLISHERS P.O.Box 1212, New London,
   Conn. 06320
Wimb   WIMBLEDON MUSIC INC. 1888 Century Park East, Century
   City, Calif. 90067
Yo   YORKE EDITION 31 Thornhill Square, London N1 1BQ, England
Zan   G.ZANIBON Piazza dei Signori 24, Padova, Italy
Zim   WILHELM ZIMMERMANN Franfurt am Main, Germany
Zsch   VERLAG Von PAUL ZSCHOCHER Hamburg, Germany

APPENDIX III
REPERTOIRE LIST

ADLER (Oxf) Canto II (b trbn)

ALSINA (Bote) Consecuenza

ANDERSON (See) Expressivo

ANDERSON, T.J. (Bote) Minstrel Man b trbn b dr hi-hat cym (all by 1)

ARNOLD (Fab) Fantasy

BACH-Brown (int) 6 Cello Suites same by Loeb (Bill)

BACH-Marsteller 6 Cello Suites in 2 bks

BACH (Led) 4 Cello Suites edited by Katarzynski (in bass clef) edited by Lafosse (ten and bass clef)

BASSETT (Ph) Suite

BATES (Ph) Tango after Clemens non Papa

BAVICCHI (Ens) Preludes

BEER (Bote) Challenge 1974

BERIO (As) Sequenza V

BERNSTEIN (SchG) Elegy for Mippy II

BLANK (As) 4 Comments (b trbn)

BLICKHAN (See) Bon mot finesse (avant garde)

BON (Am) Canzone (av gde)

BOZZA (Led) Graphismes study in contemporary graphic notation

BRINGS (See) Prosa

BRINK (BrP) Exegesis (b trbn)

BUSS (Sm) Camel Music

CAGE (Pete) Solo for sliding trbn

CHILDS (Pr) Sonata

CLINARD (Sha) Sonata

COPE (BrP) 3 Pieces (b trbn) BTRB (avant garde)

CUOMO (Med) Dry Ralph (av gde)

DAVIDOV (Ph) Caprice (b trbn)

DEASON (See) Sonoma

DEDRICK (Ken) Lyric Etude (b trbn) Prelude and March (b trbn)

DIEMENTE (See) Hosanna II (with tape rented from publisher)

DUBOIS, R. (Don) Music for a Sliding Trombone (b trbn)

ENGLUND (EdFa) Panorama

ERICKSON (See) General Speech

EVERETT (See) Natural 'D' (b trbn)

FAUST (Fau) Sonata for bass trbn

FELDER (See) Nexus (b trbn)

FRACKENPOHL, ed. (Ken) Studies on Christmas Carols

GABRIELLI, D. (Uni) 7 Ricercare

GABRIELLI, D. (SoNY) Ricercare

GLOBOKAR (Pete) Exchanges (av gde)

GRAHN (See) Trbn Unaccompanied?!

GREEN (Ph) Suite

HARTLEY (Pr) Sonata breve (b trbn)

HEUSSENSTAMM (Dorn) Trombonly

HEIDER (Pete) D.E. Memorial (b trbn) (Duke Ellington zum gedenken)

HIDAS (EdMB) Fantasia

HIDAS (EdMB) Meditation (b trbn)

JOHNSTON (BrP) Revelstoke Impressions (b trbn)

JONG (Sch) Aanraking (Contact) (av gde)

KAVANUAGH (Fisc) Debussy
  Variations No.13 (av gde)
KOCH, E. von (Gehr) Monolog 8
LEEUW (Don) Music for Trom-
  bone
LEITERMEYER (Dob) Posaunis-
  simo
LOEB (Bran) Variations
MARIE (Am) Labyrinthes (av gde)
MITSUOKA (Ph) 2 Moments Ptera-
  dactyls (av gde)
MOLINEUX (Sha) Manipulations
MORECKI (Ph) Pulsars (av gde)
NATRA (IsM) Sonatina
NIEMAN (Gen) Tongs & Bones
OAKES (See) Fantasy for Buccina
  w prepared tape
ORTON (ALM) Ambience (av gde)
  b trbn & tape (tape not included)
PEHRSON (See) Approaches
PERSICHETTI (Pr) Parable
PETERS (Euro) 14 Concert Studies
PETERS (KSM) Rondo
POWELL (BrP) Inacabado (b trbn)
PRESSER (Ph) Partita
PRESSER (Ens) Suite with fanfares
PRESSER (Pr) 3 Folktales (b trbn)
RAHN (Ph) Progressive Etude (b
  trbn)

RAPH (AR) Caprice (b trbn)
RAPH (Fisc) Rock (b trbn)
REINHARDT (Is) Music for Trbn
  Solo (b trbn)
REUTER (Int) 5 Concert Studies
  same (Zim) same (Bel)
RIDDLE (See) Soliloquy
RIDDLE (MusW) Solo Sonata
ROSS (Boo) Prelude, fugue and big
  apple b trbn & tape
RZEWSKI (EdMo) Last Judgment
SACCO (Ost) Tuba mirum (b trbn)
SANDSTROM (Nordi) Disjointing
SCHROEDER (Ger) Sonate
SHUMAN (Wein) 2 Gymnastics
SHUMAN (Bel) 5 Prep Studies
STOUT (Ph) Proclamation
STUTSCHEWSKI (OR–T) Mono-
  logue
TANNER (Dor) Etude
TELEMANN (Fisc) 12 Fantasies
VALLIER (Cho) Fantaisie
VAZZANA (Ph) 3 Monodie
VOBARON-Ostrander (EdM) 4
  Solo Suites
YOSHIOKA (Ph) Extase
YUHAS (Noga) Episodes
ZBAR (Heu) Contacts (av gde)
ZORI (IsM) 10 Pieces

Trombone in chamber music

ALBAM (Ken) Escapade solo b
  trbn fl ob cl hn bn
ALBERT (Med) Sound Frames
  trbn ob alto sax vibr (avant
  garde)
ALSINA (Bote) Trio 1967 trbn vc
  perc (av gde)
ATOR (See) Duo (with percussion)
BACHELDER (Sha) Piece
  b trbn perc

BALADA (Gen) Cuatris trbn fl/vn
  cl/va pf
BERTALI-Hill & Block (MusR)
  Sonatas a 3 Nos. 1–3 trbn 2 vns
  org
BIALOSKY (See) 6 Riddles
  (Symphosius) trbn vc voice
  2 Songs b trbn sopr
BIBER-Janetzky (MusR) Sonata a
  3 trbn 2 vns continuo
BLICKHAN (See) Quintet trbn

alto fl va pf perc

BOZZA (Led) 3 Essais trbn
perc

BRETTINGHAM SMITH (Bote)
O rise fl trbn hpch pf perc vc sc

BRINGS (See) Burlette fl cl trbn

BROWN,A. (See) Additions (Av
gde) trbn and flute with tape
delay

BROWN,N.K. (See) Hopkins Set
trbn and bariton voice

CAMPO (MusP) Commedie trb
perc

CASTLE (Sm) Entrapment vn(va)
(cl) cl(sax)(ob) trpt(hn)(trbn) db
(vc) perc

CHARDON (King) Concerto for
Trbn Chamber Orchestra of Percussion

COOLIDGE (Ken) Illuminations
b trbn vibr

DEDRICK (Ken) Inspiration solo
b trbn 2 trpts 2 hns cl vc
Sonata b trbn pf perc

DELP & WEISS (See) Modo-
genesis trbn perc

DENISOW (UE) d-s-c-h clar trb
vc pf (av gde)

DIEMENTE (See) Quartet (1967)
trbn alto sax db perc

DIJK (Don) Concerto trbn vn vc

ELGAR-Slatford (Yo) Duett. trbn
db

EVERETT (See) Duos b trbn cl

FENNER (See) Study for Timpani
trbn bn vc timp

FITELBERG (Om) Capriccio fl ob
cl b cl trbn

FREUND (See) Trio trbn vn pf

GORECKI (Ars) Musiquette IV:
Trombone Concerto op 28 trbn
cl vc pf pts

HARRIS (See) Women go to heav-
en and men go to hell b trbn pf
perc

HARRISON (SoNY) Alma re-
demptories mater trbn tack pf vn
baritone voice

HARTLEY (Fem) Concertino
trbn 4 vns 4 vcs cl pf perc
Sonata da camera trbn ob 2 cls bn
Suite for 5 winds trbn fl ob cl alto
sax

HELMSCHROTT (Boss) Inven-
tion trbn cl bn (2 copies needed to
perform)

HENZE (SchM) Amicizia! (av-
gde) trbn cl vc pf perc

HIBBARD (SchE) Bass trombone,
Bass clarinet, Harp

HOVHANESS (Pete) Mysterious
Horse before the Gate trbn perc

JERGENSON (See) Shadows trbn
4 female voices pf

KAM (Sm) Go (avant garde) trbn
vc cl conductor

KNIGHT (Pr) Selfish Giant Suite
trbn fl cl

KOWALSKI (Sm) Hors d'oeuvres
trbn and soprano

KUBIZEK (Dob) Vergnugliche
Miniaturen uber eine 12 Ton-
reihe trbn vn cl bn

LANERI (See) Esorcismi No.1 (av
gde) trbn cl voice va perc

LANZA (Boo) Acufenos 1 trbn
fl/pic cl/e flat cl vibr/cel pf

LaROSA (See) Coming in Glory
trbn alto sax vibr

LAYTON (SchG) Divertimento
trbn vn cl bn vc hpchd perc

LIEB (Ken) Song & dance trbn
strg quartet

LOVE (See) 3 impressions trbn
(doubling euph) perc

MAROS (Nordi) Spel cl trb perc
vc (av gde)

McCULLOH (Fisc) Concertino for
Large Trbn & Small Orch trbn
hpch pf

McCULLOH (See) Protagony
trbn 4 perc pf
McKENZIE (MusP) Song for
Trombone & Percussion
MELLNAS (Ton) Per Caso trbn a
sax vn db perc
NELPYBEL (Jer) Counterpoint
No.2 b trbn perc
PATTERSON (Wei) Rebecca trbn
vn vc any ww pf perc sc
PERSICHETTI (Pr) Serenade No.
6 trbn va vc
PICHAUREAU (Cho) Seringa b
trbn db/pf
PICHAUREAU (Rid) Marine
trbn vn pf
PREMRU (MusR) Concertino
trbn fl ob cl bn
PRESSER (Pr) Jorepi trbn cl pf
RAVEL (EdM) Pavane trbn hp
REYNOLDS,R. (Pete) 'From
behind the unreasoning mask'
trbn perc tape (hire only)
ROSS,R. (Uni) Tabloid ten sax
trbn
SCHMELZER-Minter (MusR)
Sonata a 3 trbn vn bn continuo
SCHMIDT (WIM) Concertino
b trbn fl ob cl hn bn
SCHWADRON (Ken) Short Suite
trbn cl

SCHWARTZ (Fisc) Areas fl cl vn
vc trbn pc pf dancers sc
SCHWARTZ (Med) Signals trbn
db
SELMA y SALAVERDE (SchM)
XXIII Canzon a 2 Bassi trbn bn
pf sc
SHERIFF (IsM) Music trbn 3 fls 2
obs enghn 3 cls 3 bns pf db
SMITH (Sm) Here and There any
mel instr pf short-wave radio
SPEER (MusR) Sonata & gigue 2
vns trbn pf
STEWART (See) Toccata sonore
trbn fl pf
STIBILJ (BA) Condensation trbn
2 pfs perc
SYVERUD (See) 4 Pieces trbn
perc
TEZAK (Tez) Dialect (av gde) cl
trbn db perc pf
WALLNER (Schul) In modo
classico 2 cls trbn/bar
WECKMANN-Lumsden (MusR)
Sonata a 4 trbn ob vn bn con-
tinuo
WEST (MS) Largo & allegro trbn
2 vns va vc
WILDER (Ken) 3 Vignettes for
Trbn trbn pf marimba fl ob cl hn
bn

Trombone and piano

ABSIL (Gerv) Berceuse
ABSIL (Sche) Suite
ALBRECHTSBERGER (EdMB)
Concerto for alto trbn
ALBRECHTSBERGER (Ros)
Concerto in F major
ALEXANDER (IsM) Shur Dodi
ALEXANDER (Gen) Sonata
ALFVEN (Gehr) Notturno eleg-
iaco (orig for cello & pf/org)
ALMILA (EdFa) Suite

ALSCHAUSKY (Benj) Konzert
No.1
AMBROSIUS (HofL) Sonate
AMDAHL (MusH) Elegi
AMELLER (Led) Hauterive Irish-
cante (b trbn) Riviere du loup
AMELLER (Hin) Dryptos
AMELLER (EdPh) Olivet
AMELLER (Bill) Ohio (ele) Utah
(prep)
ANDERSEN (HanW) Sonatina

ANONYMOUS (Fred) Sonata
ARRIEU (Amp) Mouvements
ARRIEU (Bill) Conte d'hiver
AUBAIN (Led) Aria, scherzo et
  finale
AUBAIN (Am) Theme et varia-
  tions (b trbn)
BACHELET (Int) Concertpiece
BAERVOETS (Mau) Impromptu
BAEYENS (Brog) Introduction et
  cantabile
BAKALEINIKOFF (Bel)
  Meditation Andantino cantabile
BARAT (Fisc) Andante & allegro
  same (SouT)
  same (Int)
  same (Led)
  BARAT (Led) Piece in E flat
BARRATTO (Bara) Andante
  cantabile
BARBOTEU (Cho) Prelude et
  Cadence (b trbn)
BARILLER (Led) L'enterrement
  de St.Jean (b trbn) Hans de
  Schnokeloch (b trbn)
BARON (Baro) Nirvana
BARRAINE (Gras) Lamento
BARRAINE (Job) Chiens de
  Paille
BARTLES (Fox) Elegy (b trbn)
BARTOLOMEO (Ph) Fantasia
BASSETT (King) Sonata
BAUDRIER (Bill) Relax
BEACH (As) Suite
BEAUCHAMP (Led) Cortege (b
  trbn)
BECHER (Gro) Capriccio
BECKLER (See) Sonata
BEHAR (EdMB) Concerto
BERGHMANS (Led) Concertino
  La femme à barbe
BERLIOZ (Pr) Recit and prayer
BERTHELOT (Led) Le roi
  renaud
BERTHOLON (Led) Varietes

BESSONET (Bill) Comme un air
  d'opéra
BIGOT (Led) Impromptu
  Variations
BITSCH (Led) Impromptu (b
  trbn) Ricercare
BLATTER (Med) 5 Sketches
BLAZHEVICH (BIM) Concerto
  No.1 (Int) Concerto No.2
  Concert No.5 Concerto No.10
BLAZHEVICH (Bel) Concert-
  piece No.5
BLEUSE (Cho) Acclamation
BLOCH (BroB) Symphony
BODA (King) Sonatina
BOERLIN (Sha) Multi-moods (b
  trbn)
BIOZARD (EdMT) Diptyque (b
  trbn)
BONDON (Esc) Chant et danse
BONNEAU (Led) Capriccio Fant-
  aisie concertante
BOUTRY (Led) Capriccio
  Choral varie
  Concerto
  Trombonera
  Tubaroque (b trbn)
BOZZA (Led) Ballade
  Allegro et finale (b trbn)
  Ciaccona
  Hommage a Bach
  New Orleans (b trbn)
  Prelude et Allegro (b trbn)
  Theme varie (b trbn)
BREUIL (Bill) Essai (beginning)
BRINK (Cole) Concerto
BROWN (Led) Meditation
  Recitatif, lied et final (b trbn)
BROWN,N.K. (See) Postures (b
  trbn)
BROWN,N.K. (BrP) Sonata
BRUCH (Int) Kol Nidrei
BRUCHMANN (HofL) Facetten
BUCHWALD (HofL) In
  Schlagzeilen

BUECHTGER (Boss) 4 kleine Stuecke
BUESSER (Led) Etude de concert
Cantabile et scherzando op 51
same (Bel)
Phoebus variations op 87
Piece in E flat op 55
same (Int)
BUETTNER (Benj) Conzerto
CABUS (Mau) Fuga en toccata
Ballade (ten or bass trbn, specify)
CALS (Led) Piece breve (b trbn)
CAPDEVILLE (Led) Sonate concertante
CARLES (Led) Introduction et toccata (b trbn)
CASINIERE (Led) Thème varié
CASTEREDE (Led) Sonatine
Fantaisie concertante (b trbn)
CESARE-Smith (King) La Hieronyma from Musicali melodie 1621
CHARLES (EdMT) Cortège et danse
CHAYNES (Led) Impulsions
CIMERA (War) Carnival of Venice
Improvisation
CIRRI (EdM) Arioso
CLERGUE (Lem) Impromptu
CLERISSE-Smith (SouT) Idylle
CLERISSE (Bill) Poeme
CLERISSE-Voxman (Rub) Prelude et divertissement
CLERISSE (Led) Piece lyrique
Priere
Theme de concours
Voco nobile (b trbn)
CLOSTRE (Cho) Dialogue II
COKER (Pr) Concerto (b trbn)
COME (Mau) Humoresque
CONSTANT (RicP) Concerto 'Gli elementi'
CONSTANT (Bill) Plaisance

CONSTANTINIDES (See) Improvisation
COOLIDGE (Ken) Curves of Gold
COOLS (Bill) Allegro de concert
CORDS (Fisc) Concert Fantasie
Romance
CORIOLIS (Led) Aria
CORIOLIS (Bill) 4 Piecettes
4 Recreations
COSCIA (Cosc) Romanza
COWELL (As) Hymn and Fuguing Tune No.13
CRESTON (SchG) Fantasy op 42
CROCE-SPINELLI (Bel)
Solo de concours
same (Led)
CROLEY (Ens) Divertissement (b trbn)
CRYDER (Lud) 3 Vocalises bk 1
CUNNINGHAM (See) Statements
DAGNELIES (Bel) Fantaisie variee
DANEELS (Mau) Petite piece
DAUTREMER (Cho) Coulissiana
DAVID (Fisc) Concertino op 4
same by Mueller (Zim)
same by Grube (Benj)
same by Gibson (Int)
same (Bel)
DAVISON (Sha) Sonata
DEARNLEY, editor (Che) 9 Easy Pieces by Classical Composers
More Easy Pieces
DEBAAR (Brog) Legende et caprice
DEBOECK (Gerv) Fantaisie
DEDRICK (Ken) Awakening
Inspiration (b trbn)
DEDRICK (Ken) Petite Suite (b trbn)
DEFAYE (Led) 2 Danses (ten trbn)
edition by Knaub for bass trbn
Mouvement
DEFROSSEZ (Met) Concerto
DELERUE (Bill) Concerto
DELGIUDICE (Mar) Serenite

DEMERSSEMAN (Bill) Cavatine
  Introduction et polonaise
  same (Bel)
DENISOV (Led) Choral varie (av
  gde)
DENMARK (Lud) Scene de concert
DEPELSENAIRE (Cho) Ce que
  chantait l'aede
DEPELSENAIRE (SchF)
  Impromptu
DEPELSENAIRE (EdPh)
  Jeux chromatiques
  Legende nervienne
  Le vieux berger raconte
DEPREZ (Mau) Piece de concours
DESENCLOS (Led) Plaint-chant et
  allegretto
DESPORTES (Bill) Des chansons
  dans la coulisse
DESPORTES (Fisc) Fantaise
DESPREZ (Mau) Fantaisie concer-
  tante
DESTANQUE (Led) Romance en d
  mineur
DEWANGER (Led) Humoresque
DHOSSCHE (SouT) Invocation
DOMAZLICKY (Ger) Concerto
DOMROESE (Boss) 2 Epigramme
  6 Kleine Stuecke
  Kleine Suite
DOMROESE (Led) Les ours
  Sakura impressions japonaises
DONAHUE (Tem) Bagatelles
DONDEYNE (Led) Cantabile et
  caprice
DORSSELAER (Bill) A longchamp
  Le grand Duc
  Introduction et allegro martial
  Pour la promotion
DORSSELAER (Mole) Jericho
DOUAY & GOUINGUENE (Bill)
  Divertissement
  Theme et variations (ele)
DOULIEZ (Brog) Andante op 53
  Introduction et andante

DUBOIS (Esc) Si trombone m'etait
  conte (b trbn)
DUBOIS (Led) Cortege
  Cornemuse (b trbn)
  Concerto di L'irrespectueux
  2 Marches
  Pour le trombone preparatoire
  Pour le trombone elementaire
  Pour le trombone moyen
  Suite
DUBOIS (Rid) En coulisse
DUBOIS (Bill) Histoire de
  Trombone
  Menuet d'automne
DUBOIS,T. (Int) Concertpiece
  same (Led)
DUCKWORTH (pr) Statements
  and interludes (b trbn)
DUCLOS (Led) Doubles sur choral
  Sa majeste le trombone
DURAND (Rid) Parcours
DURAND-AUDARD (Led)
  Dialogue (b trbn)
DUTILLEUX (Led) Choral,
  cadence et fugato
DUTTON (See) Music
DVORACEK (Pan) Invenzioni
ECCLES (Int) Sonata in g minor
ECKARD, editor (Pr) Highlights of
  Familiar Music
FARINA (Car) Sonata al divino
  claudio
FASCH (McG) Sonata
FAYEULLE (Led) Bravaccio (b
  trbn)
FELD (Gen) Concerto
FICHE & PICHAUREAU (Bill)
  En vacances (beg)
FIEVET (bill) Legende celtique
FICHE (Bill) Ballet pour un
  kangourou (prep)
FILLMORE (Fisc) The Trombone
  Family
  Bones Trombone
  Bull Trombone

Hot Trombone
Lassus Trombone
Mose Trombone
Sally Trombone
Shoutin Liza Trombone
Slim Trombone
Teddy Trombone
Lassus Trombone plus 14 other
trombone rags (includes all of
Trbn Family & more)
FINGER (Jim) Sonatines
FISCHER (Ken) Here I sit in the
deep cellar
FRACKENPOHL (Ac) Pastorale
FRACKENPOHL (Ken) Variations
on a March by Shostakovich
FRANCK (Sal) Fanfare, andante et
allegro
FRAZEUR (Ens) Divertimento
FUSCHS (Kr) Variationen
FUHLISCH (Siko) Schwarze Augen
GABAYE (Led) Complainte
Special
GABLER (Benj) Metamorphosen
GAGNEBIN (Led) Sarabande
GALIEGUE et DUPIN (Led)
Quelques chants 4 bks
GALIEGUE (Led) Essai I
Essai II
Essai III
Essai IV
GALLET (Bill) Legende
GALLOIS-MONTBRUN (Led)
Aria
GARDNER (SchL) Romanza
GARTENLAUB (Bill) Rite (prep)
GARLICK (See) Sonata b trbn
GARTENLAUB (Rid) Essai (b
trbn)
GAUBERT (Fisc) Cantabile et
scherzetto
GAUBERT (SouT) Morceau
symphonique
same (Led)
same (Int)

GAY (Mau) Theme et variations
GELDAGE (Int) Contest Piece
GENZMER (Pete) Sonate
GEORGE (Ac) Concerto (b trbn)
GIFFELS (SouT) Sonata
GILLIS (Bel) Dialogue
GIORDANI (Ken) Caro mio ben
same (EdM) called 18th century
air
GISTELINCK (Ande) Koan II
GLUCK (EdM) 2 Classic Airs
GOEYENS (Kjos) All 'antica
GOLDSTEIN (Fox) Colloquy
GOTKOVSKY (Bill) Concerto
GOTTWALD (Fisc) Fantaise
heroique
GOUINGUENE (Bill) Air Concerto
Ostinato
GRAEFE (Fisc) Grand Concerto
same (Benj)
same (Int)
same (Bel)
GRILLAERT (Mau) Amoroso
GRKOVIC (KaWe) Sonatina
GRONDAHL (Sam) Concert
GRUBE (Benj) Concertino
Walzer Rondo
GUERINI (StPR) Presto
GUIDE (Led) Suite: les caracteres
du trombone
GUILMANT (War) Morceau
symphonique op 88
same (SchL)
same (Int)
same (Bel)
HANSEN (See) Aria
HARRIS (Lud) Tortoise and Hare
HARTLEY (Fem) Arioso (b trbn)
Sonata concertante
HARTLEY (Ph) Capriccio
HARTLEY (Pr) Sonorities III
HARTZELL (Sha) Ballad for young
cats
Egotistical elephant (b trbn)
HASSE (Rub) Suite

HENRY (Led) Mouvement (b trbn)
HENRY (King) Passacaglia and fugue (b trbn)
HERF (Leu) Konzertstueck
HESS (Helb) Capriccio op 57
HIGUET (Mau) Larghetto ed allegretto
HILGEMAN (Col) Baroque is back
HINDEMITH (SchM) Sonata
HLOBIL (Pan) Sonata op 86
HODDINOTT (Oxf) Ritornelli
HOFFMAN (SouT)
  The Big Horn (b trbn)
  Trigger Treat (b trbn)
HOOF (Met) Divertimento
HOROVITZ (Nov) Adam-Blues
HOUDY (Led) Largo et toccata
HOVHANESS (Pete) O world
HUGHES (See) Allegro giocoso
HUGON (EdMT) Elegie
  Introduction et allegro
HUMMEL,B. (Zim) Sonatine (1976)
HUTCHESON (See) Wonder Music IV
IMBRIE (Sha) 3 Sketches (b trbn)
JACOB (Em) Cameos (b trbn)
  Concertino
JACOB (Gal) Concerto
JACOBI (SoNY) Medititation
JAFFE (SouT) Centone buffo concertante
JAMES (Lud) Elegy
JEHMLICH (Benj) Concertino op 3
JOHNSON (SouT) Fantasy
JOHNSON, editor (Rub) Sacred Solos
JONES (Fem) Sonatina
JONG (Brog) Morceau de concert
JORDAHL (See) Canto
JORGENSEN (HanW) Suite
KAI (Led) Legende (b trbn)
KALABIS (SchM) Sonate
KELLY (Wei) Sonatina
KELLY (Pr) Sonata

KOETSIER (Don) Sonatina Allegro maestoso (b trbn)
KOPELENT (As) 4 Pieces
KOSTEK (Bour) Requiem
KREISLER (SouT) Sonatina
KREK (BH-W) theme varie (b trbn)
KRENEK (BA) 5 Pieces (b trbn) (2 copies needed to perform)
KROL (Benj) Capriccio da camera
KUBIN (Pan) Koncert
KUEHNE (Bel) Concertino
KUTSCH, editor (Zim) Posaunen Klange
LaMONTAINE (FrP) Conversations
LAMY (Led) Choral varie
LANCEN (Bill) Menuet pour un ours
LANTIER (Lem) Introduction, romance et allegro (b trbn)
LARSSON (Gehr) Concertino op 45 No.7
LASSEN (EdM) At devotions (b trbn)
LAUBE, editor (Fisc) Contest Album
LAUGA (EdM) Concerto
LEBEDEV (EdM) Concerto (b trbn)
LECLERCQ (SouT) Concertino No.1
LEDUC (Mau) Arioso et danse
LEGRON (Bill) Grave et cantilene (prep)
LEHNER (Boss) Sonatine
LEJET (EdFr) Musique
LEMAIRE (Led) 3 Exercises de style (b trbn)
LEMAIRE (Bill) Recit pour un debutant
LEPETIT (Led) Piece de concert
LIAGRE (Bill) Souvenir de Calais
LIEB (Fisc) Concertino basso (tenor or bass trbn)

LIEB (Ken) Song and dance
LISCHKA (HofL) 3 Skizzen (b
trbn)
LLEWELLYN (War) My Regards
LOHSE (Bote) Imaginations 1972
(av gde) (b trbn) (2 copies needed
to perf)
LONDON (HanW) Trbn Serenade
LONQUE (Mau) Novelette
Scherzo capriccioso
LOOSER (Henn)
Variationenfantasie uber ein
eigenes Choralthema
LOUCHER (Dur) Hialmar
LOUDOVA (Gen) Ancient Ballad
LOUVIER (Led) Hydre a cinq tetes
LUENING (Gal) Sonata
LUYPAERTS (Mau) Suite
MAERTENS (Ande) Cadenza e
allegro scherzando
MAES (Brog) Concertstuck
MAGNAN (Fisc) Concerto
MAHY (Mole) Solo de concert
MALTBY (Bel) Boues Essay
MANIET (Mau) Marziale
MANIET (Brog) Piece en ut
Poco allegro
MANZO (Zan) Concertino
MARGONI (Led) Apres une lecture
de Goldoni (b trbn)
MARTEAU (Spr) Morceau vivant
MARTELLI (Esc) Dialogue (b
trbn)
Suite op 83 (b trbn)
MARTELLI (EdPh) Sonate op 87
(b trbn)
MARTIN (Fisc) Elegy
MARTIN (UE) Ballade
MASSIS (Led) Impromptu
MATEJ (Pan) Informatorium
MATTHEESSENS (Sche)
Transfigurations
MAURAT (Esc) Petites inventions
MAZELLIER (Int) Solo de

concours
same (Led)
McCARTY (Ens) Sonata (b trbn)
McCLAIN (SouT) A Little Joke
McCULLOH (Ac) Concertino No.2
McCULLOH (See) Sonata
McKAY (War) Sonata
MELLERS (SchL) Galliard
MEULEMANS (CBDM)
Concertino
MEULEMANS (Gerv) Rhapsodie
MEULEMANS (SchF) Sonnet
MEYER (Lem) Cordelineete
MICHALSKY (WIM) Concertino
MIGNION (Bill) Reverie et balade
Andante et allegro
Serenade et balade mosellanes
Cantabile minuetto
MILHAUD (As) Concertino d'hiver
MISSA (Led) Morceau de concours
MITSCHA (Pol) Romans
MONACO (Ph) Sonata
MOREL (Bill) Piece in f minor
MORRISSEY (Bel) Song for Trbn
MOSS (See) B.P., a melodrama (w
tape)
MOUQUET (Fisc) Legende
heroique
MUELLER, editor (Deut)
Spielbuch
MULLER (EdM) Praeludium,
chorale, variations and fugue (b
trbn)
MULLER (Mau) Concertino
Concerto minute
MUTTER (Moes) Chaconne (in
modo dorico) (pf/org)
NAGEL-TRUCHET (EdPh)
Impromptu
NASH (Pat) 4 Solo Pieces
NELHYBEL (Ker) Concert Piece
NELHYBEL (Gen) Suite
NESTEROV (Int) Concerto op 11
NILOVIC (Syn) Concertino

NIVERD (Bill) 6 Petites pieces de
style Chant melancolique
Complainte
Historiette dramatique
Hymne
Romance sentimentale
Scherzetto
Legende
NIVERD (Del) Maestoso et
scherzando
NOVAKOVSKY (Int) Concertino
NUX (SouT) Concert Piece
same (Led)
ORLINSKI (Boss) Konzertstuck
ORR (Nov) Concerto
OSTRANDER (EdM) Concert piece
in fugal style
same for bass trbn
On the fair grounds
OSTRANDER, editor (EdM)
Concert Album
Paris Soir
OSTRANSKY (Rub) Concertino
OTT (BenP) Toccata (1965)
PALA (Mole) Green Hills (c min)
same for bass trbn (f min)
PARES (Bill) Crepuscule
same (Bel)
PARROTT (MusR) Concerto
PASCAL (Dur) Pastorale heroique
Improvisation en forme du canon
Sonate en 6 minutes 30 (b trbn)
PAUDERT (Fisc) Fantasie marziale
PERGOLESI (Wimb) Sinfonia
PERRIN (Bill) Intro et allegro
PETIT (Led) Fantaisie (b trbn)
Wagenia (b trbn)
PFEIFFER (SouT) Solo de Trbn
PHILLIPS, editor (Sha)
8 Bel canto songs
PHILLIPS, editor (Oxf)
Classical and romantic album
PICHAUREAU (Cho) Seringa (b
trbn)

5 Concertini 'minute' (graded)
PILSS (King) concerto (b trbn)
PLANEL (Led) Air et final (b trbn)
POOT (Led) Etude de concert
POOT (Ande) Impromptu
POOT (Esc) Impromptu
PORRET (Mar) Concertini Nos.7 &
8
Concertini Nos.23 & 24
PORRET (Mole) Solo de concours
Nos. 15, 16, 29, 30, 31, 32
PRESSER (Pr) Rondo Sonatina
PRYOR (Ac) Razzazza 1–3 trbns
RAGWITZ (Deut) Sonatine
same (Bel)
RAPH (EdM) Russian sailor's
dance
RAPHLING (EdM) Lyric prelude
REICHE,E. (Bel) Concertpiece No.2
same (Int) same (Bel) Kalmus
reprint
RESCHOFSKY (Leu) Konzert-
Phantasie
REUTTER (Led) Ostinato
Etude polyphonique
REYNOLDS,C.H. (ProA) Rondo
REYNOLDS,V. (Fisc) Graphics
trbn pf (4 hands)
RICHARDSON, editor (Boo)
6 Classical Solos
RIDDLE (See) Song
RIEUNIER (Led) Silences
RILEY (Sha) Textures
RIMSKY-KORSAKOV-Gibson
(Int) Concerto
same by Beversdorf (StPR)
same by Leloir (Bill)
same by Perry (Boo)
same by Shuman (Bel)
same by (Bel) Kalmus reprint
RIVARD (Pr) Sonata
RIVIERE (Led) Burlesque
ROBERT (Bill) Air noble
ROGISTER (Bosw) Concertino

REPARTZ (Fisc) Andante et allegro
ROPARTZ (Int) Piece in E flat min
  same (Bel)
ROSS (Boo) Concerto
  Cryptical triptych (b trbn)
ROTA (Ricl) Concerto
ROUGERON (Bill) Piece en fa
  (prep)
ROUSSEAU (Fisc) Piece
  concertante
ROY (King) Sonata
RUEFF (Led) Concertstueck
RUEFF (Led) Rhapsodie
RUSSELL (Bour) Jovian Sonatina
RUSSELL (Gen) Sonata in 1 mov't
SACHSE (Int) Concertino
  same by Hansen (Benj)
SAEYS (Mau) Ballade
SAINT-SAENS (Dur) Cavatine
SALZEDO (Led) Piece concertante
SAMAZEUILH (Dur) Evocation
SANDERS (War) Sonata in E flat
SANDSTROM (Nordi) Inside (b
  trbn)
SCHAMPAERT (Met) Fantaisie
  dramatique
SCHENKER (Pete) 5 Bagatellen
SCHEVENHALS (SchF) 2 Pieces
SCHIBLER (Henn) Blues
SCHIBLER (Ahn) Signal,
  Beschworung und Tanz
SCHIFFMAN (SouT) Concert
  Piece
SCHIFFMAN (Benj) Konzertstueck
SCHMIDT (WIM) Variations on
  'St.Bone'
SCHMUTZ (Lud) Sonatine
SCHODLEY (Glo) Vocalise
SCHOEMAKER (Gerv) Piece
  concertante
SCHRIJVER (Sche) 6 Petits
  morceaux
SCHRODER (HanW) Andante
  cantabile

SCHWARTZ (SouT) International
  Folk Suite
SEMLER-COLLERY (Esc)
  Fantaisie lyrique
  2 Pieces breves (b trbn)
SENON (Bill) Chevauchee
  Melodie
SERLY (SoNY) Concerto
SEROCKI (Pol) Concerto
  Sonatina
SHEPHERD (SouT) Nocturne &
  rondolette
SHERIFF (IsM) Piece for Ray
SIEKMANN (See) Concerto
SIMONS (Fisc) Atlantic Zephyrs
SKOLNIK (Pr) Little Suite in A flat
SMITS (Met) Capriccio
SOLOMON (SouT) 2 Contrasts
  Dramatique (b trbn)
SPEARS (Ph) Recitative
SPILLMAN (EdM) Concerto (b
  trbn)
  2 Songs (b trbn)
SPISAK (Led) Concertino
STEKKE (Gerv) Variations
STEVENS (SoNY) Sonata
  Sonatina
STOECKIGT (PrMV) Sonatine
STOJOWSKI (Int) Fantasy
  same (Led)
STONE (Boo) Variations (orig f
  trpt)
STOUTAMIRE (Lud) Prelude &
  fugue
STRAUWEN (SchF) Capriccio
SUDERBURG (Pr) Chamber
  Music III
SULEK (BrP) Sonata (vox Gabrieli)
TAKACS (Sid) Sonata op 59
TAMBA (Led) Fantaisie
TANNER (Dor) Aria
TCHEREPNINE (Bela) Andante
TENAGLIA (EdM) Aria antica
THILMAN (Bel) Concertino

giocoso
TISNE (Led) Elegie et burlesque
TOEBOSCH (Mole) Allegro op
 108a
TOMASI (Led) Concerto
 Danse sacree
 Etre ou ne pas etre (b trbn)
TOURNEMIRE (Led) Legende
TOURNIER (Rid) Aareme
TOWNSEND (Pr) Chamber
Concerto
TREVARTHEN (Ph) Sonata
TROMBEY (Mole) Burlesque
TROWBRIDGE (Op) Chromatico
TUROK (See) Concert Piece
TUTHILL (King) Concerto
TUTHILL (Ens) Fantasia (b trbn)
TUTHILL (Fisc) Phantasy Piece
UBER (Ens) Autumn Sketches
UBER (SouT) Ballad of Enob Mort
UBER (Ken) Delaware Rhapsody
UBER (Ken) Golden Leaves
 Evensong
UBER (Bel) Mississippi Legend
 Panorama
UBER (EdM) 4 Sketches
UBER (SoNY) Sonata
UGA (Bill) Promenade
VACHEY (Led) 2 Interludes
VALLIER (Rid) Aria
VANDERMAESBRUGGE (Mau)
 Prelude et danse
VERREES (Gerv) Piece concertante
VETACHECK (Ph) Prelude

VIDAL (Led) Solo de concert No.2
VILLETTE (Led) Fantaisie
 concertante (b trbn)
WAGENSEIL (UE) Concerto
WAGENSEIL (Mue) Konzert
WALKER (Gen) Concerto
WASSILJEW (HofL) Konzertstuck
WATSON (Sha) Sonatina
WEBER,A. (Led) Allegro
 Concerto
 Soliloque (b trbn)
WEEKS (King) Triptych
WEINER (Bill) Phantasy op 42
WERNER (EdMT) Libre episode (b
 trbn)
WEST (MS) Largo & allegro
WHEAR (Lud) Sonata
WHITE (SouT) Sonata
WHITE (BrP) Tetra ergon (b trbn)
WHITE,D.A. (Sha) Dance and Aria
 (t trbn or trbn & pf)
WHITNEY (Bour) Cortège
WIGY (Mau) Legende
WILDER (CFG) Sonata (ten trbn)
WILDER (Marg) Sonata (b tbrn)
WILDER (Ken) 3 Vignettes
WILKENSCHILDT (HanW)
 Caprice
 Impromptu
ZAGWIJN (Don) Esquisse
ZBAR (Led) Jeu 3 (b trbn)
ZIMMERMAN, editor (SchG)
 Solos for the Doublebass Player
ZORMAN (Noga) Cells

Trombone and organ

BROWN (Led) Meditation (pf/org)
CALLHOFF (Ger) 4 Meditations
 (av gde)
CESARE-Smith (King) La
 Hieronyma from Musicali melodie
 1621 (pf/org)
HUTCHESON (See) Patterns

KOETSIER (Don) Partita op 41/3
KROL (Bote) Sinfonia sacra
MULLER (Zim) Gebet
MUTTER (Moes) Chaconne (in
 modo dorico) (pf/org)
NELHYBEL (Euro) Sonata da
 chiesa No.3

READ (King) De profundis
  Invocation
SCHIBLER (Eul) 'Audiens

exaudieris'
SCHIFFMAN (Benj) Intermezzo
SENON (Bill) Prière

Trombone and orchestra

ALBRECHTSBERGER (EdMB)
  Concerto for alto trbn and strgs
ANDRIX (SchG) Free Forms for
  bass trbn and strgs
BLOCH (BroB) Symphony
GABAYE (Led) Special
GRONDAHL (Sam) Koncert
HAYDN,M. (EdMB) Divertimento
  in D (8th & 9th mov'ts for solo
  trbn)
HAYDN,M.-Sherman (Dob)
  Larghetto P–34
HOGG (MusG) Concerto solo pt
HOVHANESS (King) Concerto
  No.3
  Diran (The religious singer) (strgs)
HOVHANESS (Pete) Overture op

76 No.1 (strgs)
LARSSON (Gehr) Concertino op 45
  No.7 (strgs)
MARCELLO-Fote (Ken) Sonata
  III (strgs)
McCARTY (Ens) Sonata for bas
  trbn and strgs
McCULLOH (See) Concerto
NILOVIC (Syn) Concertino
PRESSER (Pr) Rondo (strgs)
SCHWAEN (Deut) 4 Intermezzi
  (strgs)
SEREBRIER (SoNY) Variations on
  a theme from childhood (strgs)
SEROCKI (Pol) Concerto
SIEKMANN (See) Concerto
WAGENSEIL (UE) Concerto

Trombone and band

BARAT (SouT) Andante et allegro
DEDRICK (Ken) Awakening
FRACKENPOHL (Ac) Pastorale
GUILMANT (ProA) Morceau
  symphonique
HARTLEY (Ph) Capriccio
HARTZELL (Sha) Ballad for young
  cats
LARSSON (Gehr) Concertino op
  45/7
LEYDEN (Ply) Concerto for Trbs
LIEB (Fisc) Concertino basso (tenor
  or bass trbn)

MALTBY (Bel) Blues Essay
MICHALSKY (WIM) Concertino
NELHYBEL (Ker) Concert Piece
OWEN (Whal) Variations
PRYOR (Lud) Annie Laurie
PRYOR (Fisc) Thoughts of Love
  Blue Bells of Scotland
RIMSKY-KORSAKOV (Bel)
  Concerto
SHIRE (Ken) Autumn
SIMONS (Fisc) Atlantic Zephyrs
TANNER (Dor) Aria